The Narcissist Discard

Learning what happened, why it happened,
and how to move on, and most of all,
how it had nothing to do with you

Michael Persico

NEWMAN SPRINGS PUBLISHING
320 Broad Street
Red Bank, NJ 07701

First originally published by Newman Springs Publishing 2023

ISBN 979-8-88763-222-3 (Paperback)
ISBN 979-8-88763-223-0 (Digital)

Printed in the United States of America

Contents

Acknowledgments

I would like to take this opportunity to thank so many people who helped me along in my journey. My partner, Sarah Craven; Kevin Connelly, my spiritual mentor; Tom Ferro, my longtime elementary school friend; the golfing clan; and Eileen Itgen, who told me the truth to my face when I did not want to hear the truth, just to name a few.

I would like to give special mention to Sally and Doug, who saw me through some very tough times and helped me reach the other side. You find out who your true friends are in your time of need and when the chips are down. You will not need to ask for help. They will see you in need and be there for you. And you see the people who you thought would be there but were not.

Introduction

Narcissist! Such a powerful word. A word that sounds so vicious, so demeaning, so cold—a word often heard but many times used incorrectly and misunderstood.

For most people, it means a person who is into themselves, is conceited, and often brags and thinks highly of themselves. Usually, the narcissist is an overobnoxious male who thinks the world of himself, who is self-absorbed but highly insecure, and who could always get the conversation turned onto themselves to show how great of a person they are. This can be correct. But there is a wide range of narcissism in the world, and this is only one form of the disease.

Everyone knows a narcissist. Well, everyone knows several narcissists. There are many of them. This mental disorder strikes the wide spectrum of people from rich to poor, fat to skinny, and every religion and race. And everyone knows the unfortunate survivors or the victim of narcissistic abuse. There are many of those people too.

From covert and overt to grandiose and everything in between, like any other disorder, there is a spectrum to narcissism, and people often will fall into somewhere on this spectrum.

I want to focus on covert narcissism in a loving relationship. This is the one I did the most research on, and the one I am most familiar with. There are other forms of narcissism such as parental narcissism, employee narcissism, or sibling narcissism; but if that is what you are looking help for, this is not for you. Most of the behavior with this mental disorder is often similar, and all forms of narcissism and understanding on how to deal with this are comparable. Finding exactly what one is dealing with is important. Covert narcissism in a long-term relationship is a topic I am most familiar with. I have years of experience with this, and I have done an incredible amount of research on it.

For many years, it was believed that narcissism was a male-dominated dysfunction, and this disease was only directed at men. But in recent years, it has been discovered the breakdown between male and female narcissism currently stands at fifty-fifty. Men tend to be more openly narcissistic or show narcissistic traits more openly than women.

But women are more liable to be more covert and hidden. Yes, it is true. It was recently unveiled women are just as likely to be a proclaimed a narcissist as a man. It is because women tend to be quieter and more covert than men. Women tend to be less aggressive, quiet, out of the spotlight, and more conscientious of the way they appear. But it has been proven that women tend to be more directly and guilty of covert narcissism. Women tend to be a bit more behind the scenes and undetected. They tend to be more manipulative and thereby behave in a sneakier and more covert way.

In the past, men in many cases did not come forward after they were a victim of narcissistic abuse as to not show shame or weakness. In many cases, victims of narcissistic abuse do not realize they are being abused. But recently, because of today's communication, with social media and support groups, many men are showing just as much pain and suffering as women. They are now more probable to open up and display the pain and suffering they have endured. And for good reasons, too, because it is helping them to heal.

The pain they have endure sometimes is incredible and often dealt with for many years. Many times, what occurs is a loss of reality. The victim loses sight of what is normal and what is a fantasy world in the narcissist's head.

Narcissism is a mental disorder. And like other diseases, there are various levels or degrees to the disorder. It is not an on-off, black-white situation.

As annoying as an overt narcissist can be, a co narc can be much more dangerous, much more devious, and much more damaging. This is because they are often capable of flying under the radar and do their damage without detection. They are excellent in camouflaging themselves and their intentions in our society. They will often confuse, abuse, and mislead their victims. And unfortunately, most of the time, they cause mental and emotions damage to their victims and for the most part do not care. The fact they are covert means most victims go for a good deal of time not knowing they are being abused. The changes occur slowly from a wonderful loving relationship to an unhealthy, strenuous one.

They will come on strong, showing to be a loving and kind person, someone whom you believe could be a perfect mate for you. They will make you feel special, and as you get comfortable with them, they will want you to trust them. They will start to learn your faults and weaknesses. They will suck you in and make you have that unconditional trust in them. This is because you will gain a bond with this person. You will fall in love with them, and sadly, you will trust them. As you will learn later, this is a bad move, a really bad move.

Once the co narc gains this trust, they make you feel comfortable. After some time, as the relationship matures, they slowly change into a person you simply do not recognize. When you are not being the partner they want you to be, they will change. The damage they can inflict can be silent but serious. They will leave you feeling alone, disoriented, and confused; and they will keep you off balance. That is their secret: The more they keep you off balance, the easier it is to keep you under their control and the easier is it manipulate you. The easier you are to be controlled, the more supply you can offer them and the more they can exploit you.

You will live and breathe for them. Remember, this will become all about them as long as their needs are met.

It is sad, but the truth is that they will never gain a bond with you. That bond that two people who really love each other gain. You are nothing more than a possession they have now, a possession which is not supposed to think for themselves or disobey. You are for them only, someone who only lives and feed the co narc's unfillable needs. And an important point here is, it is an unfillable need.

You are not a partner nor a special companion to them; you are simply only a possession, like a pair of shoes or a cell phone.

After speaking to several people who also had long-term dealings with a co narc and who were eventually discarded by a co narc, the co narc becomes very addictive. They are incredibly good at sucking you in and making you feel special, making you feel that you cannot continue without them. After they have hooked you, they will find and exploit all your faults and then they will pound you and beat you mentally, emotionally, and sometimes physically.

Unfortunately, they will become relentless and never-ending. They will never compromise, nor will they ever give quarter. And because you are exactly what they were looking for—a good giving person, a person who is strong and stable, one who will always give to the last ounce—unfortunately, you will continue to take the punishment, even when most people who are not so nice would not. They are attracted to you because you can give a good deal and not take. The co narc purposely chose you because you are a strong, confident, and a successful person. You are person they want to be. You have qualities they so desperately wanted. They chose you because you can pick them up. You will make them look good at first. You will make them feel good, and most importantly, you will fill their need.

They look to you to be their savior. You will for the near future and give them the fill that their fragile egos need. They are like a hawk looking for the perfect mouse to pounce on. They, on many occasions, bypassed many subpar preys. They rejected the not-so-ripe fruit because they knew that fruit was not able to give them what they needed.

They do not pick a person who they find weak or unable to provide what they are looking for. They do not want someone they must raise up or give supply. The fact of the matter is that the relationship with a co narc becomes very quickly impossible and is bound to fail. This is because it almost always becomes a one-way relationship— from the victim to the co narc.

The co narc does not want to give; they only want to take. They do not want for any attention given to anyone but themselves. They just want to take and take. As I have learned, and I have learned this the hard way, this is no way to live. It is not enjoyable, and sadly, there is absolutely no way there could be a good outcome. It will end badly. Period.

After some time, if the victim does not get tired and leave, the co narc will almost always leave the victim in the discard, and they will leave when the victim when the victim is the most vulnerable at the most inopportune time.

The co narc will discard when they are unable to suck anything else out of the victim. They will leave when the victim needs them the most and when it is most advantageous to the co narc. Remember, the narcissist does not want to give; they just want to take. And the saddest part of this is they do not care. They do not care about the victims' well-being, feelings, or emotions. When they leave, they will want to not only leave the victim, but they must destroy them.

They will not want the victim to be able to recuperate and be able to move on and do better and move on faster than they could. They will not show any empathy or remorse. This is the co narc at their worst, the hidden demon that now shows their hand—the person nobody expected or a person nobody who knew them would believe was possible to exist. But they do. That is why they are so dangerous. It catches the victim off guard, and it can be devastating to the victim.

After the discard, the co narc will do an incredible job to hide the damage they have caused over the entire relationship. They simply cannot let it be known that they were the problem, and they caused the pain and suffering in the relationship. They will gaslight and manipulate the people close to them. They will continue to paint the victim as the aggressor and themselves as the poor caring victim that tried so hard at keeping the relationship together, even when it was the other way around.

The co narc simply does not have the ability to self-reflect on themselves, so to protect their fragile ego and to cover up their actions, they will place themselves in the right and victim in the wrong. They will blame the victim to others for everything. They will put the victim in a damaging light and a big fat halo on their big, fat lying head. They will exaggerate details and just outright lie. Manipulation is their superpower. They need to; it is mandatory for their survival.

The co narc will use the victim until the victim is of no use to them. That is when the co narc enters the discard phase. More on that later.

But what is especially important here to understand is that they were planning the discard way before they executed it. Before the triangulation and before the devaluation. It was going to happen. Just as they had planned this from the beginning. They were absorbing everything they could off you: physically, emotionally, financially, and mentally. They were learning your weaknesses and insecurities, and they were going to exploit them when it was best for them.

You had to be a strong person to deal and endure this kind of abuse for such a good deal of time. A weaker person would not have been able to endure this and have given up long ago. Or the co narc would have left; no, they would have run at the first sign of the new victim not able to give enough. But the co narcwould have known all of this before they picked them. You were strong and confident, and that is why they picked you. You had all those qualities that they wished they could possess themselves, and they will later hate you for it when the co narc realizes they are not able to be as good as you. Yes, they will hate you for it.

As you will soon discover, that was all part of their plan—the discard, as vicious and shocking as it was. After the discard, after the confusion and pain, you will realize the amount of work, energy, and time that it took for you to continue to stay in the relationship. And as you will discover, it was enormous—no, it was insurmountable. And after it all, it was not worth it all. The co narc was not the person you thought they were. You thought they were a person they were not. The person you fell in love with never existed; it was all a farce.

You could have done so much better and without all the torment, complications, and rules. They were not the great partner you thought they were, and after the discard, you will realize it was just not worth it.

After all this, it will become understandable to wonder why this all happened to you. Why you? You may start to feel sorry for yourself, but that will soon pass. You have started to learn about all about co narcs. The self-pity will soon turn to understanding and confidence. When you find out you are not alone and there are particularly good reasons to the why and what, it will soothe you and, most importantly, allow you to move on. You will realize you are a much stronger person; and the co narc, in many cases, held you back. Instead of pulling the rope in the same direction as you like a team, they fought against you and what you were trying to accomplish. Just imagine a person pulling in the same direction as you. For all that time you wasted, how far could you have gone?

We will get into why and how to break the habit and how to move on and, most importantly, how to find and get into a healthy and loving relationship.

You will enjoy it. It will be effortless; it will be enjoyable. It will be like night and day. The big neon sign will be as bright and shiny. It will be so clear. The idea of a healthy relationship will be a new beginning for you. And it will be healthy for you.

Today, about 8 percent of American adults are classified as narcissists or have narcissistic traits above a certain level that makes them harmful. Yes, that is one in twelve. One out of twelve people, male or female, it does not matter; they are a narcissist. Not just a narcissist but a person that has this mental disorder and cannot be cured. A person for whom it is not an on-or-off disorder. It is a progressive one, and the intensity varies. The numbers in recent years, unfortunately, is on the rise. Why? Some believe it is social, and some believe it is genetic. But most people who are narcissistic have had some traumatic incident that occurred to them before they reach the ripe old age of seven.

It has been shown that people who have narcissistic tendencies come from parents that also have shown signs of narcissism themselves. One or both parents will often be the barer of insecurity. Whenever a child encountered a situation, the parent or both parents of the child often will disregard the feelings or thoughts of the child. The child's feelings will often be suppressed or disregarded as unimportant, irrelevant, or incorrect.

The parent will force their own feelings onto the child or tell the child how to feel or just plain ignore them. The child matures, unable to know how to comprehend their own feelings and understand their own comprehension of situations. Most often, leaving them feeling lost, insecure, and abandoned. This mostly will lead to the co narc not being to successfully develop their own ego and set of emotions, retarding their own development both mentally, emotionally, and socially. This is often the case why most narcissist act in a childish manner. They are morally, emotionally, and socially bankrupt.

As an adult, when a situation occurs, the co narc is incapable of knowing how to connect with their feelings. They are often unable to set their own boundaries, unable to make useful decisions, unable to self-reflect, unable to make up one's mind. And oftentimes, after becoming frustrated, they will lay the blame on whomever is the closest; and that is the victim.

Not only will they be unable to handle these situations, they also must protect their own fragile egos. As a child, they were constantly being told they were inadequate, incorrect, and should not express themselves. Their ability to gain self-confidence suffered. They were unable to allow this part of their personality to mature, so a co narc will never gain the confidence in themselves as most others do. They need that constant feed and confidence others must provide. And as we had stated before, it could never be enough.

As you will come to understand, the child will not be able to function in a normal fashion nor in a healthy manner. They will not be able to trust nor be able to secure a bond that healthy people come to know with another person. They will always be seeking for someone to set the boundaries for them, telling them how to feel or what to think and fill the unfillable void in their lives, completing their lives but never really fulfilling their needs.

They will look to and copy others around them and act like them. Their trust in other people simply cannot be fulfilled. They will never be able to complete the love bond and trust others. As soon as the people around the co narc cannot fill that need or when a person around a co narc needs some sort of feed from the co narc, the co narc will discard. Remember, the narcissist only takes; they do not give.

They are incapable to gain a deep connection with not only people but also with themselves. They never feel comfortable with themselves and will eventually hate themselves.

Everyone will act narcissistic at one time or another, and we all have some degree of narcissistic tendencies in us. Yes, we all can be narcissistic at times, and we all act this way sometimes. We all have insecurities; and we resort to narcissism to defend these insecurities, when we become confused with our feelings, when we need control, or we are insecure about a certain situation. But most people do not use it constantly to manipulate and demoralize another person to maintain their own well-being, to keep that person under their control and manipulate them mentally and emotionally. And it comes into play how severe and how often the narcissist comes out of us.

A good example is when all of us can be cranky at one time or another. But the question becomes how cranky others see us. Are you cranky all the time, or do the smallest thing set you off for being cranky? And the important thing here is, does your crankiness effect other people? There is a checklist of several items that measure the degree of narcissism a person can be. The more traits checked off puts them higher on the narcissist list. As I said, we all have narcissistic traits. It is the person that is highly narcissistic for most of the time that is the one you must be cautious of, the one you need to stay away from.

Many people are subjected to covert narcissism for many years. They do not even know what it is nor that they are being abused. I found a treasure trove of information on the internet, in books, and on social media. I had to sift through a mountain of data and learned a tremendous amount of not only what people had endured but also why it happened. And there was nothing they could have done to change the outcome of the relationship.

I will say it again: There was nothing they could have done to change the outcome of the relationship. It is a long rough road. But time heals all wounds, and after some time, the victim will feel so much better than they did before. So for now, you are reading this because you were discarded by the co narc, you left a co narc, or you are still involved with one.

If you are still involved with one, listen closely. There is never a good outcome from this. The sooner you leave and cut all ties, the better off you will be. Most victims find this part exceedingly difficult. Wherever you are in the healing process, hopefully, this book will help you move on, help you heal, and more importantly, help you live a better life.

It will not happen overnight, and sometimes, things will feel unbearable. You will experience the roller-coaster effect of where, one day, you are on top of the world; and the next, you are down and out. One moment, you understand fully what you were against, feeling good; and the next day, you are feeling bad because you felt sorry for the co narc and that you could have done something different that could have changed the outcome.

But once you break the addiction, your life will turn to the better. The chains will be broken, and you will learn who you are. It may take a year or two or ten, but you will no longer be so uptight about things beyond your control. And most importantly, you will understand the boundaries that were put on you. After, you hopefully will find a healthy relationship and see how easy it is with someone who really cares about you and how effortless it is to be in the relationship. You will be you. What a novel idea.

There is a good deal of help either on the internet, support groups, or psychological/professional help. So to suffer in silence without knowledge is simply unnecessary. But sometimes, it is hard to realize you need help. A person can wander through life and not realize they have a problem. The signs are there, like a big neon sign flashing at them in the face, and they still cannot see the signs. But after they realize what was happening, it will be as clear as a bell.

As we will uncover, all co narcs act remarkably similar. They all follow the same rules from the same playbook. Learning about co narcs and their behavior is becoming more understood. And once you begin to comprehend all this, you will feel better about yourself because you will see it had nothing to do with you. The co narc tried to blame you and tried to tell you that you were the problem, and in many incidences, you thought you were. They led you to believe that. You believed their lies through manipulations and gaslighting. You tried hard to make things work, but it was an uphill battle. No, it was an impossible task. A battle that you could not win. So do not try to win, even when the co narc tries to come back. It is a battle that takes so much energy, so much time, and an incredible amount of patience.

When we finish, you will wonder why you put up with so much for so long. Why did you let the co narc push you around and, yes, abuse you? You let it happen. So get comfortable and start to move on. Leave all that in the past.

As you reflect and learn about the battles other survivors dealt with, you will see the similarities and how others dealt with them. You can compare the insanity with what you were putting up with, see the mistakes others made, and what worked and what did not.

One other thing you will dwell on is the times you may have not handled certain incidents the correct way or in a decent manner. Heck, we are all human. So do not beat yourself up. Not all experiences are the same, nor will they make any sense. But you may see the similarities. Once you start to heal, you will start to think about individual times and certain situations that occurred. And one by one, you will make sense of all the confusion. These are times that you may have forgotten or may have thought insignificant, just a simple memory that will make you see how important they are. And most importantly, they are significant to your moving on. So many of us speak your language, so listen.

What Happened?

So there you are, recently discarded. You are confused, scared, embarrassed, and relieved all at the same time. Hundreds of emotions are running through your head, each one needing thought and comprehension. The person you loved for so long had just suddenly left you without closure and usually at the most inopportune time. You would never have guessed how mean and insensitive they could be. You would have bet they would never had done this to you in a million years.

You knew there were rough spots with the relationship but did not understand the true problem. You always knew your relationship was a bit different, different than that of others in your realm of friends. People around you tried to tell you, but you did not listen, not because you did not want to but because you were blind.

Your partner not only blamed you for everything that was not always right but also behind your back to make you look bad to others. They made it look as though you were the problem and you would not change, even though you did not have to. But you stood there, constantly dodging the arrows hurled at you, jumping over the boulders rolled at you. Sometimes, you would start fighting back; why not, you got tired and had your fill.

Sometimes, you were not doing the correct thing and sometimes overreacting because after a while, you had so much bottled up inside you, it just had to come out sometime. But in all, you were trying to figure it all out and, most importantly, trying to keep it all together. You tried your best to make things work, and though things were normal relationship items, you felt things were acceptable, not great but acceptable.

You looked at other couples in your age range and did not see anything out of the ordinary. You saw there were things you had better than other couples and things that were a bit less. You are reading this because you were, or you believe you were or are, dealing with a co narc—a person whom you fell in love with, a person who made you feel wonderful, and you thought loved you.

But as time went on, the real person emerged, a person you did not recognize, a monster. This may be the hardest thing to understand and the hardest to swallow. But they are a person who not only did not love you but they also never did and never will; they simply are not capable. What you must understand here is that the narcissist wanted to love you and probably tried to love you. And they loved you as they knew how to love. But it is not the love that normal functioning people feel, and they do not form the natural bond that two loving people form. You did but they didn't.

They are a person, as we will find out, who is incapable to love. They are so empty inside, have such a lack of self-confidence and lack of self-worth, they cannot have any empathy. They are hell-bent on securing their own footing, making sure their own well-being is safe, and not giving a care about anyone around them. And they will destroy anything or anyone that gets into their way or keeps them from receiving their source of fill.

Their life is comparable to a large house of cards. They will exert an incredible amount of effort to protect that house. And if anyone dares get too close to it or attempt to it to knock it down, their wrath will emerge with an incredible fury. Any little criticism, any little comments that are against their thoughts and feelings, they will take it as an attack on that house. Your job as the partner or lover of the co narc is to help them protect that house. They found you because you are capable of it. They felt, with your confidence and ability, you were perfect for this job.

But as time passes, they will find fault with the way you protect it. You were not perfect, so you were inadequate. And when you could no longer do it exactly the way they think you should, you will be fired.

They came on strong with charisma and charm. And you being the strong, self-confident person they thought you were fell in hook, line, and sinker. That is why they chose you. They picked you because they saw your strong will and leadership qualities. A co narc will not pick a loser or someone that will require them giving any of their energy into. They are selfish; it becomes all about them.

They want someone who can pick them up and supply them with energy, and someone they know can supply them with fill.

The changes did not occur overnight. It took some time for it to start, but it happened. It came faster and more furious. You may think you are alone, the only person in the world who is dealing with this problem; and you may feel ashamed, like you did something wrong, or foolish because you were duped and allowed it to happen. You may feel like someone who is going through a situation that nobody else understands. Unfortunately, it happens more often than you think. You are not alone. Many people understand all too well what you are feeling. They have been there, they walked the same road, and they speak the same language.

Hopefully, with the help of this book and some additional research, you will figure out the things you need to know and understand on your own. Why at one moment they were so nice and sweet, the person you fell in love with; and then the next minute, you are hearing from your family and friends that they were talking badly about you, trying to destroy you and your reputation, and making you look bad. Why? It does not make any sense.

You thought you found a person who would build you up and work together to achieve a happy life, someone who will pull in the same direction as you and not hold you back or fight against you every step of the way. And often, they would come home to you with their flying monkeys (a *Wizard of Oz* similarity), telling you that all their family and friends can see what a horrible person you are, how poorly you treated them, and how they put up with you.

You stand there trying to get it, trying to figure out why they were always in turmoil, upset, and cranky all the time. Why were they always getting upset for the simplest things? But the saddest part of this all is you believed them. They were the one telling their family and friends lies about you. They were so good at manipulating, gaslighting, and making you believe you were the problem. They also were manipulating their flying monkeys. You did not realize it was all part of their lie, their deception. It was all fabricated in their head and played out with you as the star.

You are looking for understanding on what happened and why and looking for the best way for healing and moving on. You always knew there was something different with your partner, but you could not see it. Once you start to read this and start to understand the different behaviors of your partner, you will put it all together. You may have had different names for each behavior, but in the end, you will see it is all the same.

As you delve into this deeper and hear stories of other victims, you will see all the stories are similar, remarkably similar. But remember, it is like putting a jigsaw puzzle together. You may have a piece in your hand, and it just does not fit anywhere yet. Do not discard it. Just be patient. As the puzzle gets constructed, the piece may eventually fit. Not only will it fit, but it may also make total sense and make all the other pieces more comprehensible. And you will see things you did not see before.

Narcissists will almost always all act the same; they are so predictable. If you were able to change notes with another survivor of narcissistic abuse who is in a comparable situation as you, you would be amazed at the similarities they all commit. I was amazed to find out that it was so similar that when I spoke to other survivors, I felt as though they were standing in my living room observing every word and situation, taking notes.

All co narcs are empty souls, requiring a tremendous amount of attention, admiration, energy, and work. Someone once said that trying to fulfill a narcissist's need is like trying to fill a bucket of water to the top with a hole in the bottom. It is endless and futile and can never be accomplished. Unfortunately, the amount of work and energy will become impossible to provide, for as time goes on and you try to fill the bucket, the hole becomes bigger and bigger.

And because you will become tired and dispirited, the amount of water that is being poured reduces to a trickle. And once you do not provide it or do not pour enough water into that bucket, you will pay, and pay big.

Once you understand more, moved on, and healed, you will see the amount of work it took in your troubled relationship. And when you are in a healthy relationship, you will see how easy and comfortable it is and what it's like to have a partner pulling in the same direction as you instead of against it. It required a lot less work, almost effortless, and you will have to get used to it. Someone who will pick you up when you fall instead of someone laughing at you when you do.

At first, it will not be easy to let your guard down. It will take time to find out who you are, but slowly, you will.

As you think back to past times, you remember you were constantly putting out fires and always walking on eggshells, never quite sure how to act or react to situations that happen. Why you reacted one way at one time and things were fine, and the second time, you reacted the same way but caused a such a huge conflict. You stood there, thinking how you could have handled the situation differently or how you could have not seen your insincerity.

It simply could not be them. All your friends and family found them to be so sweet and kind, a person who was so generous and always had a kind word to say about anyone, someone whom everyone wanted to be around. But when you got home and the front door closed or got into the car and the doors locked, they would change into Dr. Hyde almost immediately. You now were on the receiving end of a barrage of questions and tongue lashing on your time spent.

I hope to help you understand why these things happened and how to overcome the discard when it happens. What I hope to do is make it easier for you to heal—the quicker you understand what and why this happened, why and how it was the game plan, how none of this was your fault and it was going to happen. The narcissist was planning the discard from the beginning, or at least when they realized you were not perfect.

And with that, I want to make clear that they will almost always never change. Instead, feel proud of yourself because you lasted as long as you did. You did not deserve the treatment that you received, and now it is time to move on. You now need to take some time to heal and figure out who you are and where you wish to go. It will be a rocky road, one with difficulties. But the road will become smoother and more level as you travel it and, most importantly, straighter and easier to navigate because all the ice and snow will melt. Now sit back, relax, take a deep breath, and thank God they are gone. Thank them that they discarded you. Yes, call them up and thank them. You will heal and you will do better. And you will be happier; trust me.

What I found out most interesting was how hard it was to cut the cord and move on. After years of being trauma bonded, victims become addicted to the abuse. They get stuck in the web of narcissism. Why would I after I found out I was abused for so many years? And what a difficult and hard life I lived. Why was it so hard to move on and live a life like so many others? The answer is simple; it is called trauma bonding. We will see why this happens and why it is so hard to break the tie you had with the co narc.

Am I a psychologist? No! Did I take psychology in college? Yes, but received less than stellar grades. So why or how could I help you? It is simple. I am knowledgeable on how it feels, why you feel it, and what these feelings mean. But the most important thing is how to get to a normal place of being again. It will take time and it will be slow, but as you walk that road, you will at times look back and see the difference. And that will motivate you to keep moving forward.

One of the most important things I learned from all this is how they cannot be helped. They will always be a narcissist. Let me say that again: There is no help for a narcissist. They will follow the same road map, and the relationship will always end the same way—badly. The worst part is that there will be no closure, no understanding why. Therapy, medication, or promises will not work. There is no cure for these people even if they wanted one.

So do not be fooled when they want to come back. Yes, I said when they want to come back, they almost always do. And they tell you that they are sorry and they will change, they understand why the relationship did not work, and they see they were the one with the problem. They may be sorry and they may want to change, but they cannot. There is no known cure yet known for them. Do not listen to their empty lies, as tempting as it may be and as badly as you may have been trauma bonded. They will not change even if they wish they could, and in the end, you will only be hurt again.

So protect yourself and do not be a fool. After giving many victims advice on narcissist survivor websites and after speaking with other survivors, whenever the survivor took the co narc back, even after they were warned by many people, 100 percent of the time, the survivor was hurt again. So heed the warning and do not fall for their empty promises. Do not take them back. It will be a guaranteed failure.

Confusion

If you were in the relationship for a long time, you took some time to look back at different incidences and tried to compile through your thoughts all the craziness, insanity, and the good times. You replay instances when the co narc was upset with you or uptight about something you had no control over or when you were sometimes trying to be the person they wanted you to be.

At the time, you would reason, *Oh, had I just not gone to the store at that time, had I just realized that the towel in the bathroom was wet, had I just bought the correct brand of bread, had I just not asked the pretty girl behind the counter for change of a dollar, or had I just not recommend we go to the beach that day, my ex would not have been upset with me and we would have had a great time.* You say to yourself, "I screwed up. I caused the problem."

Well guess what: You were a victim of trauma bonding and gaslighting at its finest.

But now, you must realize, and it is important to comprehend this, that no matter what you did during all those times, or what you said, or what you did not say or what you did not do, you were going to get it. It was going to happen. It had nothing to do with you. They just found a reason to strike out at you because something happened that hurt their fragile ego.

The co narc picked out of left field, something they were going to hit you with. The big red button in their head which controlled the insecurity realm was pushed. And once it is pushed, it cannot be released until someone gets hurt. They will now find a need to strike out. And where do you think they are going? They will always strike at the easiest target. The target they know they can get away with. You!

You become the punching bag. It is that simple. Somebody either got too close to knock down the big house of cards or did damage to it, something you were not in control of but were going to be blamed for. Not directly, but you know it was coming. It was something his sister said to him at dinner, or was it that she put on a pound or two over the last week and her pants were a little tight, or he was criticized because he could not park his car correctly?

And there you are, sitting there FDH (fat, dumb, and happy) when suddenly, *pow!* You got it. But you will now realize it did not matter. They were gunning for you no matter what, and anything you did or said was going to set them off. They were going to find fault with you and or anything you did or said. It is due to their own insecurity. It made them feel better striking you, and it also let them pound their chest because it showed they still had total control over you and the situation.

They are a hollow soul. Again, a hollow soul that can never find its fill. But you were being the empath, so you put the Everlast shirt on and took the punches. Maybe you fought back, maybe you did not, but you are at a huge disadvantage because you have no idea what is going on. You are playing defense, trying to figure out what the problem is. And they are riled up and focused but you are not. You are not in the mood to have a confrontation, but it found you.

They are passionate, and you want to just watch TV. You are sitting there without a problem. You are trying to sit back, watch the game, or drink your beer. But believe me when I say it had nothing to do with you. You were not the problem; you did nothing wrong. You were simply the one in their crosshairs. You were the easy target. They hit you because they knew they could get away with it. And it made them feel better hitting you. The dopamine in their head gets released, and they feel good. They have control, and that is what it is all about.

That is where a major problem starts for the victim. The victim becomes gun-shy. They will start living a life, always thinking of how not to make the co narc angry at them and how not to make them upset. It unfortunately will become a way of life. The victim will start walking on those eggshells barefoot, constantly thinking, *What do I do or not do to not make them unhappy?* It becomes extremely tiring, taking an incredible amount of energy and time. And as it will be realized, it will never be right.

Unfortunately, the victim becomes a different person. A person and the people around them who know the victim will start seeing a person they do not recognize. The victim is not living a life they may want—happy and healthy—and it will show. This is all part of the abuse. This is the worst kind of abuse—the silent kind, the mental abuse and the emotional abuse. The victim does not have any visible scars, but the inner scars are the worst because they are the deepest and take the longest time to heal, if they will ever heal at all. These are scars nobody can see, so they have no idea what is going on.

The victim becomes wounded. They are wounded, and it was all because of the co narc. And most importantly, the co narc does not care. They have no compassion, no empathy. The victim will begin being short with people. They will be afraid to say anything or do anything. The victim will be on a playing field that is strange to them. That is not fair to them nor the people around them. They become put under a spell.

So after the victim and the co narc separate, the victim will find peace and they will not have to walk on those eggshells. They will become comfortable again. Human.

One might often say, "Why did the survivor just not leave?" I often said this about battered and abused women. Why would they stay with a person who hurts and belittles them all the time? A battered woman is not just physically abused; they are more harmed by the mental and emotional abused. The survivor of the co narc is also.

As I found out, the answer is not so easy.

After some time, many survivors who are dealing with a co narc may begin to think that this kind of behavior is normal. They lose sight of reality and what a healthy relationship is. And there are trauma bonding and gaslighting involved. There are finances involved and, in many incidences, children to think about. Also, after a bad incident or situation, the survivor believes this time that when the co narc struck, it was not so bad and they seriously believe times will get better. If only they stay calm and use logic. Maybe try a little harder to make them happy.

But I found out, the problems did not get any better, and because the victim surrendered, it only emboldens the co narc. It only gets worse. Now the co narc knows a way to win. It gets worse because the co narc is learning how to strike harder and they become more comfortable and more efficient at it. And then they blame the victim for it. They hone their skills to razor-sharp edges, and their venom becomes more potent. The victim will slowly relinquish their power, and the problem will snowball out of control.

In the beginning, the victim was the deal. The victim was the knight in shining armor. They saw the victim as an incredible place to get that supply they so desperately needed. No matter what the victim did or did not do, the co narc saw them as a perfect match. The co narc praised the victim and would do anything to get them.

Times looked promising, and the relationship looked bright. But remember, the co narc is an expert at manipulation and they have a sick and unhealthy agenda. They feed off victims' energy, and they are studying their every move. They will say the things that they believe the victim wants to hear, as well as do things that they believe they want them to do. A person who quickly learned the victim's weaknesses at the drop of a dime would later strengthen the co narc's position, and the co narc will exploit them against the victim to gain control.

All that because the victim screwed up. They made a huge mistake; they trusted the co narc. They mold themselves to the person they believe the victim wants. After some time, the victim becomes whipped. But unfortunately, the co narc did not look at the victim to build a two-way, fifty-fifty relationship with. They looked at them, looking at what they could suck off of the victim. What is in it for them? That is all.

And because they have become experts at manipulations, the victim becomes dependent. This becomes the place where the victim wants to stay or later get to. But they will take every weakness and thought the victim had, and they will. Sometimes in the future, when the victim is most vulnerable and when the victim is looking for some support, needing someone to lean on, they will pull out that weakness and use it against the victim when the victim is not expecting it, when the victim is looking for comfort.

Yes, it will happen. That is mental abuse. And they have no remorse or empathy. They, in a sick way, will feel pleasure at the victim's misfortunes. They are so miserable that they feel good when a good person is in pain, when something bad happens to the victim. It's crazy and insane but true.

Unfortunately, this stage will not last forever. In fact, it will not last exceptionally long.

But when things begin to break down, the victim begins to remember the good times in the relationship, the times when they felt what the relationship was all about; and it brings them joy. The chemicals in your brain aligned, and that is where the victim kept trying to get to, wishing they could go back to those times because the victim is a good person, an empathetic person. They tried so hard to make things work.

The problem was, those times were so far and few; they were rare. And it is important to realize they are experts in manipulation and the victim became the glutton for punishment. The victim still loved the person and still wanted them. They were so afraid to think about moving on. It seems so unsettling. The victim may not have any place to go, or they have children with them.

But unfortunately, those enjoyable times with that person the victim thought they loved did not exist. That person was not real, and those times were fictitious—all fake. It was all a charade. The co narc is an expert in acting the way they believe the victim wants. That is how they baited the victim.

Do not feel bad, but you were duped. It happens to the best of us. If the co narc was not so good at manipulation, they could not exist. It is the lifeline of their survival. So they become particularly good at it quickly!

As the relationship progresses, the victim starts to see changes. But they did not believe their senses, or they did not trust them. It simply cannot be so. The victim and the co narc start to argue a little bit more and start not to agree completely. The co narc becomes belligerent and start to set boundaries and rules. At first, the rules are simple, like putting the toilet seat down or the way they park their car.

But as the relationship advances, the rules become more numerous, more controlling, and more bizarre. Remember, this is a slow process, and the rules come so it is not noticed. But the victim keeps putting it off and continues to move forward. The co narc, as the relationship is progressing, is learning the victim's strengths and weaknesses and are setting the boundaries according to the victim's weaknesses. They figure out what works and what does not work, and when it works, they will exploit the situation. And once a boundary is set into place, it is set in stone. It becomes very difficult to move, change, or omit that rule. Once it is set, it is set.

So as the relationship matures and the number of rules increase, the victim very quickly realizes there are rules for them but none for the co narc. Whatever rule or request the victim may have or ask them to follow, it simply cannot be accomplished. They will simply not do what the victim asked them so nicely, and the excuses will be incredibly lame. *Oh, I spent so much on the dress because the sky is blue.* Well, maybe not that lame, but you get the idea.

Remember, co narcs cannot have boundaries and will not care about anything the victim requests. The victim's needs are not important. But God forbid the victim step out of bounds and breaks one of their many rules. Whether it was not wearing shoes in the house to the inability to watch certain TV programs to not being able to go to certain places.

But after the discard, one of the things that you will realize is that it was a tremendous amount of work and effort to follow all their rules and requests to keep the relationship upright. The victim started to walk on eggshells because they simply did not want to hear the co narc or feel their wrath. Again, not a good way to live your life; and if you are the victim, the number of rules became so numerous and complicated, you will forget three-quarters of them or were simply unable to follow all of them.

And as crazy as it is sometimes happening, the rules will overlap, such that it turns out if the victim does one thing like breaking a rule or doing the opposite thing, they break another rule, so much confusion, so much tension. So they are damned either way they go. But again, think about all of energy it took or is taking to keep the co narc satisfied. And the point here is since we have learned the co narc cannot ever be satisfied, the rules are becoming more complicated and impossible to follow.

And sometimes, the victim will do something or an incident will happen, and even though the victim did not break a rule or step out of bounds, the co narc will claim you broke the rule and make up a new rule as it happens. And the victim should have known you did a bad thing and would step out of bounds. It became tough, but the victim kept trying.

Part of the rules and requirements from the co narc the victim was bound to fall short was in the realm of the gift giving. Again, as the relationship is in the initial stages, any gift the victim gave the co narc was a winner. The co narc loved the gift, and it was perfect. It was the perfect color and perfect size, and how did the victim know that is exactly what the co narc wanted? They made a big deal of it and showed it off to all of their family and friends. And the victim felt good.

But as the relationship progresses, the gifts become less and less significant. The gift was too big, too small, or not the right color. The victim will try harder and harder to get the right gift, only to be disappointed almost every time. It was at this point that the co narc would say something like, "You never put any thought into your gifts," or "You know I do not like the color beige." This is quite hurtful after the victim tried so hard to please the co narc. Again, the victim will soon notice it is taking tremendous amount of work and energy when it should not.

It will get to the point where any gift the victim gets for the co narc just before the discard was never right. There may even come a time when the victim receives rules for gift giving. Again, just like the number of rules that increase during the relationship, the rules for gifts and gift giving increase also. And the rules become impossible and bizarre.

Pocketbooks, perfume, sneakers, sweat suits, boots, and jeans, may be the items the victim were forbidden from getting the co narc. After going crazy trying to purchase the right gift, there will always be a problem with it. The point here is the victim will go through so much trouble, spending so much energy, money, and time. But unfortunately, the victim will fail. Yes, they will fail no matter what. But because they are probably trauma bonded at this point, the victim will not give up and only try harder next time.

What a victim may later notice after the discard is that they gave 1,000 percent more energy on their gift than the co narc. They may become so focused on trying to please the co narc, they will not notice how lame the gifts they received were. And whatever the co narc got the victim, the victim was satisfied with it because they love them.

One thing the victim may notice is the gifts they started to receive over time become less thoughtful, selfish, and insignificant. They will see the gifts the co narc got for others, such as a friend of theirs or family members, will be very full of thought; and the victim cannot help but to notice their demeanor when the co narc gives that person the gift. They will have a smile on their face, and their eyes will glisten, just like when they did when the victim was in the love bombing stage.

Another thing that many victims notice is the gifts they will start receiving will be items such as a romantic dinner or a couples massage or tickets to a show. The co narc is now receiving part of the gift they gave. Remember, it is all about them. They need the control, and they do not want to give anything. And now, they do not want to make the victim happy. They are just pretending to care. And trust me, the victim will feel it and it will hurt. But as always, the victim will make excuses and open themselves up for more pain. And it will happen again.

So now with all the rules and regulation and the boundaries set with the gift giving, the victims walk around with their guard always up and ready to try to satisfy the co narc and make them happy in any way possible or, in many cases, just try not to piss them off. Again, tiring and never enough. But the worst part is the victim is now becoming a person that is not the person they are or want to be. Since they are walking on a tight rope, they become off balance, unstable, confused. And this is how the co narc wants the victim to be. Now the victim is easier to control; they are behaving.

Now you find yourself emotionally all alone. You become addicted to the narcissist, under their spell. Why is it so hard to give up on something that is hurting you so badly and is so tiring? Why do you keep hiking uphill, steeper and steeper trails, only to realize you can never get to the top of the hill?

You can move on, and you will move on. It takes a little bit of time, and understanding will help.

The fact you are reading this book means you are hurting badly like so many. Suddenly, your life is thrown upside down. The day the co narc discards you, you did not want them to leave. It is shocking. The change in events happens overnight. Now, I hope to help you understand what happened, what to do to heal yourself, and realize not only it was nothing you did or did not do but the person you fell in love with. Well, that person never existed.

Something that is impossible to see right away will become clear. A person who purposely tried to hurt you and tried to beat you down. A person who was jealous of you, who enjoyed seeing you fail, or gained delight when sad things happen to you. A person who, during the entire relationship, did not pull that rope in the same direction as you but instead fought against you every step of the way. The person who came on so strong with the love and attention in the beginning suddenly disappeared. A person who never loved you, not because you were not lovable and not that they did not want to but because they did not know how to love you and was unable to.

And here is the truth, they never will be able to. You will read this and think that I was sitting in your living room watching all this. How could I know what happen to you and your relationship? How predictable were their actions? But believe me, co narcs all act the same. Very predictable. But the real thing here that is the basis of this whole writing is there is no cure for the co narc, no gallons of medication, no training, nor hours of therapy. I did not believe it at first, but it is true.

If you are in a narcissistic relationship, you may think you can help the partner or, over time, the narcissist will or can change; but you will only be spinning your wheels and wasting your time. The fact is, as the co narc gets older, they will only become more insecure and will become worse, not better. Heed the warning. Run fast, run far.

So many tried. So many have been down that road before you. So right now, sit back, relax, and thank God they left. They just did you a huge favor. You will be happier. Your life will become much more enjoyable. You will see that there is so much more to life, and life does not require so much energy.

There will still be rough spots and growing pains, times that you will think about things that you wish were still happening with the co narc. You will think about the good times, and it will bring a smile to your face. But in a brief period, people around you will tell you that they have never seen you so happy. And you will agree because you will feel it.

Blindsided

Discarded. Some people just cannot believe it when it happens. Even after a tremendous amount of time, most victims simply cannot believe the co narc discarded them. Most victims will admit that deep down inside, they knew it was going to happen but are still surprised when it does. Surprised because the co narc probably went through one of their temper tantrums before, sometimes several times. *Why was I discarded?* After many years, the victim was still the same person. Why now?

Most victims will admit it was like walking down a long tunnel, then they see a light at the end of the tunnel. They can hear the train coming, and the light keeps getting bigger. The vibrations will become stronger and stronger. And still, the victim just stands there, like a deer in the headlights of an oncoming car. You hear the sound getting louder and louder, then slam! The train hits them with full force.

The victim will not even know until months after it happened, nor what they were dealing with. They knew they were a good partner or at least in the realm of a normal partner. But according to the co narc, the victim was the most undesirable human being who ever lived. Everything wrong with life was the victim's fault. The victim did not provide them with what they needed or wanted.

As you will realize, a co narc cannot be cured and certainly cannot find true happiness. I wish to help anyone going through what I know is an exceedingly challenging time. I know the pain and suffering you are in. I will tell you there are times of total confusion, total bouts of loneliness, and mountains of pain. But healing takes time, and time will help. But the more you research what the problem was, the easier and quicker the healing will occur. It will calm you down and make you realize you are going to be okay. And the most important thing to remembered is that it had nothing to do with you. You got into a situation that firstly had nothing to do about you, and secondly, you could not fix so you fell out of control.

Now this does not mean that you were totally innocent, and this does not mean you handled every situation the correct way. I am sure there were times you handled things in a less than stellar manner. We are all human, and we make mistakes. So if you can recall an incident where you were a little bit under total control, do not beat yourself up. You were dealing with a demon that the best minds in the world of psychology could not figure out nor repair.

You were up against something that is impossible for you to understand or comprehend. So how could you, being a totally innocent bystander, expect to come out on top or even be in the running? It was the narcissist presenting a problem you could not only not handle because you were unprepared and not trained to deal with this mental disorder but was also forced to deal with a situation that is not winnable.

You were forced to fight a fight when you wanted to go for a gentle walk. You fought a fight on their grounds with their rules. There was no way you would be able to cope with this because you were not able to do so, and nobody would expect you to. So under no circumstance should you think you could have done any better than you did in this engagement. My point is this: Seek help when you are hurting and do not understand things, and give help when you feel you could help anyone you see is a poor soul in the same situation.

Remember, you speak that strange language that only narcissist survivors understand. Do not only speak it; shout it out loud. Unfortunately, you're in the club. It's not a chosen club but one that can make a difference because this disorder is not going to go away anytime soon, and your experience in this subject can really make a difference to someone else out there who is fighting that impossible fight that you know all too well.

It is important to understand that there are three phases of narcissism or covert narcissism. Each one is very definitive, and there is a cycle between all three. Some occur quickly, and some take a good deal of time to ferment. But they all happen, and they are very definitive and distinct. And understand this. Some occur and then advance to the next level but then would cycle back and forth, and unfortunately, this is all part of the confusion.

The victim will never quite know which phase they are in. As you walked down this dark and mysterious road, you may have noticed the different ways the co narc acted. The victim may have come up with different terms for each of these stages, but you will see the official terms for these behaviors and you will match them up with what you have dealt with and how similar it was for what you put up with and endured.

The three phases are the love-bombing phase, the devalue phase, and finally, the discard phase. There is usually a good amount of movement between love bombing and the devalue stage. This is usually dependent on the mood of the co narc. Times will go from the love-bombing stage to the devalue stage, back to the love-bombing stage, back to the devalue stage and so on. And at times, you will advance to the discard stage. Congratulations, you are a member of prestigious but rare group. As we will discuss later, this will not be a pleasant place where you will want to be.

But the co narc will truly not be finish with you yet; so when they have found a way to suck a little more blood out of you, they will automatically revert back to the love-bombing stage, bypassing the devalue stage. And you will fall for it again.

Unfortunately, or fortunately, for most of the relationship, you will be in the devalue stage. Their unhappiness and insecurity will be demonstrated mostly here. During this phase, triangulation, gaslighting, flying monkeys, and straight out devaluation will also occur here. That is where the co narc will proceed to slander you and tell lies to people around you. They will also try to make themselves look like the victim, and you like the weak and useless pathetic loser you are not.

The co narc is basically making themselves the victim, and they are looking for sympathy. In order to keep total control, they will also try break up friendships that they believe would not be advantageous to their agenda. And they will slander and tell you lies about the other people so that you will dislike them. They do this to drive a wedge through your relationship with others whom they may not want you to be friendly with or they just do want to see you happy and secure. Again, the co narc is in full control of the situation. More about this later.

You will notice that your friends, colleagues, and people close to you will not be dealing with the same crazy items that you are in their relationships. They tell you tales or stories about their partners and how easy relationships should be, and you compare theirs to yours. Their partners were not doing the things your partner was doing. They were not demanding the things your partner was demanding. You see what a normal relationship is, and you view your relationship and compare because you are not stupid and you are not blind.

And what becomes very frustrating is when you tell your friends and colleagues some of the things you are dealing with at home, they simply cannot believe you. The things you are telling them seem so out whack, so impossible. They met your partner. They were very personable and a joy to be around. You must be exaggerating the situation, or you are delirious. And unfortunately, that keeps you a bit off balance because you will start to doubt yourself. You will even think it is you, and you will begin to feel very much alone.

But you will learn things that are eye-opening. As you research all about covert narcissism, many things will become clear. It will make total sense with incredible clarity. Some may think that the narcissist changes, that they come to a point where they want to discard the victim. But that is not at all the case. In most cases, it is not the co narc that changes but the victim. Yes, the victim changes. Everybody has their limits, and they come to a point where they stop trying to fill the co narc's fragile ego with compliments and accolades. They start to rebel against the nonsensical and bizarre rules, or they start to demand a leveling of the playing field with setting boundaries with the co narc.

So the victim has moved too close to that house of cards and now becomes totally useless to the co narc, the co narc starts to look for new supply. Not only will the co narc start to look to move on and starts setting up for the discard at this point because of loss of control, but they will also begin to panic. Remember, the co narc cannot be rejected. They cannot have boundaries and, most importantly, the fear of abandonment. What they begin to think is that the victim will abandon them and the victim will reject them, and this will be a huge blow to the co narc's already fragile or nonexistent ego.

That is a total breakdown of control, and they can never give that up. So to protect themselves from this unacceptable fate, the co narc must strike first. They must make the decision and keep control, and the discard is just around the corner. Now, they may not want to discard the victim. It may not be financially and physically advantageous, but they must. They cannot relinquish control. So in many times, they will bite their nose to spite their face.

They will dump you before you dump them. Again, there is no love connection here. There never was. There was no commitment and no bond whatsoever, so the co narc is moving on. They will get rid of you as if you were the old car on the side of the road with the flat tire and will not start. You were just a tool to them, and now you do not work.

What is more disturbing is they do not care if it hurts the victim or the people around them. They do not care about what is the best for children or anyone else. They will discard the victim when it hurts or causes the victim the most pain, when it is the most devastating to the victim. What is especially important is they must now destroy the victim for rebelling, for not staying in line, and for not feeding the co narc. So the victim cannot be happy after the discard. Seeing the victim suffer is rewarding to them.

It is important to note that a co narc only sees things in black and white or good and bad. What I mean is that they will only see a person and situations as good or bad. They either do good things or terrible things; there are no gray areas. So they either love you or they hate you. Just like a child under the age of four watching an old TV western. When you were in the love-bombing stage, you were the cowboy dressed in white. You were the hero always coming to the rescue. And in a flash, you became the cowboy in black, the villain always causing misdeeds and destruction.

You became the cowboy in black in the flick of a light switch. When the devalue stage started, you became bad. Not only are you bad, but everything you say and do is bad. You are a despicable human being. But when they need their fill and they can suck off you again, you became the good guy again and the one dressed in white. And you become confused.

The reason for the black-and-white perspective is that they have no core. They do not know who they are or how they should feel. They simply act in a way they think everyone around them wants them too. Co narcs have trouble handling their emotions.

A trauma occurred to them as a young child where their feelings and emotions were pushed aside and made unimportant. So they never matured emotionally and now do not have the ability to handle many situations that require emotions. Remember, they are very shallow, so they are incapable to fall in love or achieve a bond with anyone. That is why they also lack empathy.

They mirror people they admire and act accordingly. They say things that they believe others will want to hear. They lack any opinion. They do things that they think others will like and say the things they feel others will want to hear. And they do it well. This is something they have been doing for a good deal of time. They have mastered it. It has become a way of life for them.

They will suddenly like a certain type of beer or a certain type of car. They will now like a different type of music or love a restaurant that they would have never eaten in before. Why? Because someone they admired or though were aware said so. It will become law. That restaurant will be the best, the beer the tastiest, and that car the best-looking car model ever made. That same car four years earlier, when you were looking for a car, was the ugliest thing going. But understand when they were in the devalue stage, which is most of the time, anything you could tell them could not be.

Remember, you are the cowboy in black and they hate you. You are bad. So they will not believe a single word you say, and what's more is they must automatically disprove anything that comes out of your mouth. You must be made insignificant and mainly not in control. They will come out holding two dresses and ask, "Which dress should I wear"? Whichever you choose, they will wear the opposite one.

Many times, the co narc will believe anything a total stranger tells them, but anything that the victim says simply is wrong. They will try to disprove any theory the victim says or simply not like anything that is chosen. This is because they are jealous of you. They do not want you to succeed or look good, so they will do what they could to knock you down. They will never compliment you, nor will they ever be proud of anything you accomplish.

Again, this is the hollow core they have, so they will never apologize for anything they did. Yet they will require an apology for sneezing the wrong way. They will never apologize because they never self-reflect. They have no self or boundaries, so they could never be wrong. That would be a blow to their ego. And if the co narc is proven wrong, it will always be turned around to be someone or something else's fault.

It becomes amusing after a while. You will own the only house in the neighborhood where the dishwasher does not work (even though it works fine), the vacuum does not clean properly, there is something wrong with the washing machine, the stove is a piece of junk, and the house is the most hideous looking in the neighborhood. Anything you do in the house is inadequate. The paint was the wrong color, or the window you installed did not work properly. It was all your fault. And you were bad, so you grew tired quickly.

As I stated before, it becomes very tiring keeping the ship afloat. After a while, their insecurity increased, so the rules become not only more numerous but more intense and the more out of line with normal life. Your black outfit becomes blacker. And worst of all, the victim forgets who they are.

In the beginning, there were no rules. By the end, you lost count of them. No matter what you did, it was not good enough. You had rules for everything. This is the co narc taking more control. They must try to change you, and you must change. This is their control.

This is the empty core I spoke of before. No matter the compliments you gave them and all the great gifts that you got for them, so excited waiting for them to open them, they would never get their fill. So you were always disappointed and just gave up. Well, no you did not. You are being the empath, and you will try again and again. And could you guess the outcome then? You became a glutton for punishment, and you deserved it for being so foolish. But there it is.

There Is Nothing Wrong with You

As it was mentioned before, a co narc is an empty soul. With that, a narcissist must always tell you how they feel. Their feelings are what is important, and no matter what your feelings are, they are unimportant. So do not even try to express them. This is all part of their insecurity. You could sit for hours every morning, listening to the co narc talk and ramble on about this or that. You would pray for the phone to ring or someone to knock on the door. You had to provide your total attention to them when they spoke. And God forbid you interrupted them or interjected something or looked in another direction. It was met with, "You never let me talk." That is a narcissistic injury. That is met with narcissistic rage.

The next day, they would start talking again and mostly say exactly what they did already, and you must just sit there and look interested in what they were saying.

You sat there. You tried to be a good partner. You really hated these times. This would be supplemented by the times they came home and they had to tell you about their entire day. They would often get upset if you did not ask them how their day went. You often chose between them being mad at you or sitting for an hour and listening to their garbage.

One point I wish to make here is you can think about all the amount of energy and time you put into the relationship. No relationship—well, no healthy relationship—should take so much energy and time. Yet you could not hold the co narc's attention for more than five seconds. Your ideas and your wants just were not important. It did not matter. Anything that you may tell them that is important such as retirement funds, people at your job, or banking or insurance, which was just not important; and they shut you out. You are unimportant; only they matter.

But one thing many have learned is to not ever criticize the co narc or tell them of their faults. Narcissist do not take criticism well. Once you expose them or tap one of their insecurities, they will act in an irrational way. They are so insecure, so hollow; they will sometimes respond with rage. Many have seen that rage. Sometimes, it was physical, and sometimes it is suicidal. So be careful and tread lightly.

They also need to have their flying monkeys by their side. A flying monkey is a person, whether it be a friend or family member, that they use to manipulate to make them see you are a horrible person. Just like when the co narc was manipulating you, they used gaslighting and all the other tactics to either drive a wedge between the flying monkey and you or for the flying monkey to think badly about you.

Sometimes, one of those flying monkeys will attack you because they were to believe the co narc's lies. They were led to hate you too. It is very similar to the wicked witch in the *Wizard of Oz*. The witch did not go out herself and do the dirty work against Dorothy; she sent the monkeys to attack. For the co narc, they will often do the same sinister plan. They often will be nice and sweet to the victim or be acceptable when, behind the victim's back, they are slandering and blatantly outright lying, making up things about the victim.

These will be friends, family members, or coworkers of the victim. Now think of this. The victim at home, when they are around the co narc, is walking on eggshells, not being the person they are comfortable being. And when around these flying monkeys, the contact with these people will not be harmonious and will not comfortable, so the victim is not living a happy, comfortable life. And it is all because of the co narc.

Many times, when around the co narc and the flying monkeys, whether it be at a party or some sort of get together, the co narc will often wish to stir things up a bit. Remember, they know exactly which strings to pull to get under the victim's skin. They sense the perfect time, and they will strike at the most inopportune time to the victim.

Unfortunately, the victim may react in an imperfect way. Often, they will either overreact or react on a less than perfect way. I often make the analogy, just like in a football game, when the players start pushing and shoving after a play. It is not the player who throws the first punch who catches the penalty; it is the player who reacts with the second punch that the referees catch. And then the yellow flags come out, and the second player gets the penalty. It is he who looks bad and out of control. At that point, the co narc will sit back and act just like the player who threw the first punch, putting up their hands and saying, "Look at them. They are out of control, and I am just standing here."

During most of the relationship, the narcissist is jealous of you. They hate when you succeed and love when you fail. They will not show it, but they will be smiling on the inside when things do not go your way. That is why they are covert, which is why they are so dangerous. You are not their partner; you are their possession. They own you. You are like a brand-new car to them. You do a service for them, but they do not love you.

When that car starts to get old or breaks down, they hate you. They have no emotional attachment to you. You are there for them, you are there for their purpose, and you are there to fill their void. Again, they are a void that cannot be made whole. So when they realize you simply cannot fill that void or you change and stop trying to fill that void, they will start to devalue and triangulate you. Eventually, they will discard you. They never get that bond with you, a bond when two people fall in love for each other. They are incapable of it. And I will say it again, and this is the truth: There is no cure. They would purposely try to make you fail. Most of the time, they will do it behind the scenes quietly. Again, covertly.

Also, you cannot say anything to them as a criticism because that is a big no-no. It is countered with a quick, fast, and often vicious response. Let's say the co narc knew the victim was a stickler for bills and credit cards and paying them off on time. The co narc goes out and spends money out of control, buying things that they necessarily may not need or overpaying for items they easily could have purchased cheaper.

The co narc knows it would bring the victim pain and discomfort because of the victim's need to keep the bills under control, so when the balances could not be paid off or credit problems occurred, it would bring a sick pleasure to the co narc because even though it was not beneficial to both, it hurt the victim more. Remember, misery loves company.

And should you confront the co narc about the bills or overspending, it will be met with attacks and counterattacks. Remember, the co narc cannot have boundaries. So after a while, the victim just gives up.

That is what you are dealing with—a person not in touch with reality. You cannot succeed. Good things cannot come your way, and the co narc will make sure of that. You're the salmon swimming upstream, and the waterfall is lined with hungry grizzly bears.

Also, should you get any awards or acknowledgments, the co narc will make it as though it was not big deal. And they will show everyone you really did not deserve that achievement.

On the other side, their accomplishments better be acknowledged with an enthusiastic congratulations. If not, then you will hear it. They will say, "Everyone at work thinks I am great worker, and I do a great job. Everyone loves me, but I come home and I do not get any appreciation." Yes, you could compliment them repeatedly, daily, hourly; but it will never be enough. They will never hear it. It is like trying to fill that bucket with a large hole in the bottom with water. Impossible.

The Love-Bombing Stage

As always, when you meet someone and start to date, you're always on your best behavior. The true you will not come out just yet, nor will the true them. But first dates are always awkward. As the second and third dates occur, the real you will start to emerge. The fake them will emerge, and you become more comfortable. But the co narc will be observing you intensely.

They picked you for a reason. They not only chose you because you are attractive to them and you had an enthusiastic sense of humor but also because you exuberated confidence. You have what they want to have, and more importantly, you are what they want to be. They saw you as someone who can pull them up. They were not thinking on building a relationship with you with love and compassion. They were looking to suck what they can off you and move on. Yes, they are hoping that you will feed their ego and build them up.

The co narc saw wonderful qualities that you possessed that they wished they had. Your ability to interact with people, the way you had feelings toward others, the way you loved and used your emotions—they saw these qualities wished them for themselves. You had things and qualities that they wanted or wished they had. They watched you in the beginning, how you walked into a room full of people, the way you greeted others, the way you showed your positive energy, the way you are comfortable in your own skin.

Remember, they simply have no core. They do not like themselves. They do not have this positive energy, so they really do not know how to do any of this. They soon will become jealous of you, and soon, they expect you to exuberate these qualities on them and only them. They did not want you to use these qualities on others. Remember, you are there for their benefit. You must act the way they want. They want to take those qualities from you. When you did use these qualities on others, they become jealous and they will begin to resent you.

They will begin to hate you because you are the person they want to be, and now the attention is on you and not them. They want to take these qualities from you, but they cannot. So they will start to devalue you. They will say to you how badly you behaved or how badly other people see you or that you were embarrassing. It is sad, but they want to break you. Their jealousy comes out, and they know they cannot do the things you do. So now, you cannot do those great things. Again, they hate you. And when a co narc cannot control you, they will damage the way others see you. So they will devalue you.

You showed them you were successful. You see, in the love-bombing stage, the co narc will see you in an amazing light. They will be looking for someone to fill their endless ego. They will emulate you. They will act the way they believe you want them too. They will cook for you, buy you nice gifts, and do special favors for you. They believe you are special so they will see you as a perfect mate, someone who can take them to a place they wish to go. They believe you can fill that void in their soul, which nobody before could fill, so they will do anything that they believe will make you happy.

Remember, they are an expert in manipulation. They must be to survive. They have no foundation to feed against. They are emotionally immature. They will act the way they believe you want them to. They will dress to a tee and always look their best. When you meet, they will always have a smile on their face and arms open to greet you. Anything you buy for them, any restaurant you attend with them, any movie you go to see will be perfect. They will introduce you to people with an enthusiastic dword.

They will feel proud to be with you, and you will feel it. And as I said before, the gift giving will be extreme. But most of all, they will overlook any of your faults and flaws. I will not say if you had faults and flaws, but because we all have faults and flaws, they will overlook any of these you may have and continue to see you as a perfect mate. And most incredibly, you will feel good. They see you in a way that is simply not real. Then they want to live in that fantasy world. They believe you will be perfect. So this person, in every way that they become is not real; they are fake. Everything about them will be false. They change from this stage is amazing. They were a different person, so much so they are simply unrecognizable from their original self.

I wish you to remember that since this is an enjoyable time, a time when your partner is in a good place, this is where you try to go or return. This is a person who is an expert in manipulation, and they are incredibly good at it. But unfortunately, they just discarded someone else. They just moved on from someone else that they became tired of, or someone just saw into them. A co narc becomes bored quickly. Very quickly.

When the co narc engages with a group of people, they will adhere to the person whom they feel will benefit them the most. They will ignore the person who may be nice and friendly but worthless to them. They sometimes will rotate between people as situations change. Again, it is all about them. It is all about what is in it for them.

As soon as the person they are with fails to fill that unfillable ego, they are moving on. You are now their new savior, and they will swell your head. They will make you feel special. You are now the cowboy in white. You like being there. You like being special. They will now mirror your actions and act in a way that they think you want them to. They will say the things they believe you want to hear. They will talk to their family and friends about you. It will all be positive because, remember, they are insecure; so they found something amazing.

They will try to make themselves look good because they found someone special. You will be the highlight of her conversation and actions. If you were a Michigan fan and they were an Ohio fan, they would put Michigan banners in their room. Again, the chemicals in your brain will align, and this is where you want to get back to. But often, it is rare. But these are the times you remember.

After a brief period, they will then see you wearing the black cowboy suit. And this love-bombing phase will end. But in the future, when they either need you or need something from you, they will revert to the love-bombing stage. They remember and know just how to pull those strings to trick you back into the love-bombing phase. And you will fall for it every time or at least you will try to be the good partner.

Even if the co narc has moved on from you, when they need something or when they feel you could be useful to them again, they will hoover you. Or in other words, they will love bomb you again. And the problem is that you will get confused. You will not realize where they are or where you are. This cycle will go from high to low in a matter of minutes. It is not uncommon for a co narc to be in the devalue stage for weeks, then you will see the change in them in a moment.

You see it in their face and in their attitude. And unfortunately, when they are in this stage, you will do anything to keep them there. You will be walking on eggshells. You will stop breathing to keep her happy. But as you will find out, it has nothing to do with you. You will be the punching bag. You put up with it because you are a good person. Unfortunately, this cycle could go on for months and, in some cases, for years. After a while, when you are dealing with a co narc, you may start to believe all this is normal behavior.

But the question comes up. Does the co narc know they are acting in an unusual way and strange manner? The co narc knows exactly what they are doing, and they know it is wrong. They are incredibly good at hiding it. They will wait until the car door closes, the company goes home, or they hang up the phone, then Mr. Hyde comes out. And they will be incredibly good at controlling when they act up. Particularly good. But not perfect.

They sooner or later will mess up and usually at an inopportune time for them. Remember, you cannot hide the crazy all the time. It will come out. And that is how you know that they are in full control. They realize the difference between right and wrong. If they did not, then they could not turn it on and off with such ease. They know what they are doing. They are in full control of themselves. Trust me, they must be for their own survival.

The Devalue Stage

The devalue stage comes into play when the co narc realizes you are not the perfect partner they previously thought you were and you are not playing the game the way they thought you would. You are not filling that unfillable need that they so desire; you are not fitting the mold the perfect way. Not only that you are not the perfect person, but you also do not see them as the perfect person.

You are not going around telling everyone how fantastic they are. You are pointing out flaws that the co narc has. Remember, there is not a gray area with a co narc. They only see in black and white, so if they feel that you do not think they are the perfect person, then they believe you think they are a bad person. This is very damaging, causing narcissistic injury to them. Part of the problem with this is they are afraid that since you do not believe they are perfect and they have many flaws, you will reject them.

You will eventually discard them. They believe you should have thought they did no wrong. Their opinion was always correct, and since you do not, you think they are the perfect person. They are a horrible person. In their twisted mind, they believe you simply cannot love them because they are not perfect.

Now, in order to protect themselves from the shame and humility, they resort to pointing out all your flaws and imperfections. They also will believe you are telling other people of their flaws and weaknesses. So they try to beat you to the punch. But here is the bottom line.

They hate you now, and their jealous distrust for you will now emerge its ugly head. So now they must knock you down a few pegs or at least put you back into where they believe you should be. Since they cannot control you or at least you are not under their total control, they will now begin to belittle you. They will point out of anything that they believe is bad. At this point, they also know what criticism will really get under your skin.

Not only will they start to criticize you privately but also publicly. They will also begin to try to make others around you start to see you in a bad light in an attempt to pump themselves up. They will triangulate you, and they will not always tell the truth. They will do anything to make them look like the victim, like the football player who threw the first punch and waited for your reaction.

Part of what is going on here is the co narc begins to hate you. Yes, they will dislike it when you succeed and, in a sick or unhealthy way, gain satisfaction when you fail. Remember, they do not want you to do better than them. You are not supposed to take the spotlight away from them. It will unfortunately progress into a love-hate relationship. That black-and-white, no-gray-area relationship will begin, and it will become a cyclic connection.

Not that you have done anything wrong, but you are just not superhuman. But you did a very bad thing: You were yourself. And the co narc finds that totally unacceptable. They do not like it when you succeed or when you take the spotlight away from them, or at least you are not building them up to themselves or to others.

You are now the cowboy wearing black. The devalue stage is really a confusing stage for the victim. The co narc was love bombing you, and they built you up to a point in which you believed you were special in this person's eyes. You felt that the bond between you and them was developing on a normal pace, and you become extremely comfortable in the relationship.

But unfortunately, you are not that perfect person the co narc believed you were. You are not the person whom they felt could fill that void that is missing in their life, a person who could give them total control. Remember, the co narc needs to be in total control. And when they are not in total control, they will do whatever it takes to regain it. During the love-bombing stage, they are learning how to manipulate and control you. They are learning all about your strengths, weaknesses, secrets, and vulnerabilities.

They began gaslighting you and figuring out how to make you do or be the person they want you to be. They will mold you, just like working a big lump of clay. But eventually, you will step out of bounds. You will violate the unwritten rules the co narc has set in stone. Not only are you to blame, but when someone else close to the co narc steps out of bounds or they act in a way the co narc does not approve of, they will look to you to quell that person into line. When you do not because you did not think of the co narc's feelings, then that is a strike against you. You will receive the wrath of the co narc.

Since you cannot monitor everything other people do or say to the co narc or you cannot understand how the co narc will perceive things in their head, sooner or later, somebody will say something to or do something to the co narc and the co narc will look to you or blame you for not protecting them. Remember, they have a demented way of looking and perceiving things.

They have a way of twisting things around or just placing the incident into the wrong box. What may be a harmless comment or interaction, the co narc will take it out of context and they will take it as an attack against their fragile ego and make it a black item instead of a harmless gray item. And yes, you will become the punching bag. After the company goes home or after you leave the party, you are going to hear about it.

But unfortunately, you are not Superman. You will be yourself and not the person they want you to be. A time will come and they cannot control you with the methods that worked before. This cannot be. So the co narc will switch gears. They will advance to the next level and try other ways to get you to be the way they want. And at this point, they will enter the devaluation stage. And again, it is unfortunate, but there was nothing you could have done to avoid this. You could not be perfect; it's impossible. The point I wish to make here is you are not the problem, but with all this, you will begin to think how not piss off the co narc—an impossible task.

Yes, they will start to call you a slob or give the compliment of "You look fat in that outfit," or, "Everyone sees how awful you are to me." This is where the emotional and mental abuse starts. Let us face it; nobody wants to hear criticisms about themselves, especially from the person they feel a special bond with. So the victim will try to satisfy the co narc. They will go on a diet, they will not speak at the times they usually would, they will try to clean the house more, they will become a person that they are not and do not enjoy being; but they do it to try to satisfy the co narc. But it will never happen.

Remember, the co narc is exceptionally good at manipulation. They know what works and how and when to use it. They will apply whatever means necessary to get the results they want. The co narc will also try to launch flying monkeys. They will try to get others to look down upon you. This is another way of gaining control—to whip you into shape. This makes them look good and brings them sympathy. And right now, they are setting up the discard or trying to validate the reasons for the discard. Believe it or not, this is where the thought of dumping you begins. If they make you look bad, if they make you like a loser, then when they dump you, everybody will understand. They are setting the scene in their own head.

Another point here is that the co narc starts bashing you to others. Also, it takes the spotlight off you and on to them. Again, the co narc loves attention and admiration and, most of all, sympathy.

When the co narc starts to devalue you to other people around you, this also is known as triangulation. It is a little different from basic complaining about you to others because they will often bend the truth and straight out lie about you. And just like gaslighting, they are playing mind games with them. They will paint you in the most unattractive light. But many times, the co narc will not just come out and bash you in a negative way, but what they will also do is make it out as if they are caring and concerned partner.

They will say something like, "I am concerned about Joe because I think he is drinking too much," or, "I think Joe is losing a bunch of his friends because he has been very cranky lately," or, "Susan had two desserts last week, and I am concerned about her high blood pressure." They always want to look like the kind, caring person; but as you know deep down inside, they are evil, pure and simple. They do not care one ounce about you. But they look good, and that is what is important.

They will also exaggerate. If you drink a beer occasionally, you will become a compulsive alcoholic. If you leave a fork or dish in the sink occasionally, you are a total slob. This is a very popular tool the co narc uses because they believe it is an effective way to regain the control that they are so much desire to stay on top. Remember, the co narc does not see themselves in a bright light. They do not believe they are a good person, and they just do not love themselves. So they cannot have you look better than them.

They are jealous of you, so by bringing you down, it settles their already broken self-esteem. They look superhuman for being such a good person dealing with you. And what is harmful is the co narc opens the victim's vulnerable box. They will reveal sensitive and private things to anyone who will listen.

Remember, the co narc will learn the victim's vulnerabilities and weaknesses during the love-bombing stage. Many times, it is the victim trusting the co narc during the love-bombing stage, opening and admitting delicate feelings and bits and pieces. Everyone has skeletons in their closet, and this is unfair of the co narc to spread this.

This is not normal in a normal relationship, but remember, this is not a normal relationship. And the co narc will unethically spread this information to everyone who will listen. But again, you screwed up; you trusted them. Shame on you. You just wanted a lover. And on many occasions, the co narc will hate you because you love them. Yes, as sick as that sounds, it is true. They simply do not love themselves; they do not see themselves in a bright light. So you must be a really screwed-up person because you love them. You love them with all their faults and insecurities. So they hate you.

Eventually, the news of this triangulation will get back to the victim, and this can be devastating. It really hurts a great deal. The person they love, the person who is the number one in their life, the one person they thought they could trust, the one person they opened to, the one person whom they grew this bond with is betraying them, tearing them down, making them look bad. This will, again, put the victim on the defensive.

This keeps them off balance, and when the victim is off balance, the co narc is in control. At first, to the victim, this is a huge blow. Not only are they confused; they are embarrassed. Stress levels go up, and trust issues go straight out the window. The victim simply does not know what they now can say or not say to the co narc, and those eggshells come out again.

The victim will now withdraw. They will close their vulnerable box and keep it closed. Unfortunately, not only may they never trust the co narc again, but they may never trust anyone again. Again, this is simply unfair to the victim. Not only will the victim start to try to comprehend what information was given; but they will also wonder what was said to others and when, what is true, and what has been fabricated. So the victim becomes off balance, and the co narc is in control.

So when your co narc graduates away from the love bombing to the devalue or triangular stage, you often bend over backward to try to get the person back into the love-bombing realm. Remember, they are particularly good at love bombing. They are great manipulators. That fantasy world that they lived in is a beautiful place; but remember, it does not, did not, and never will exist. But you will try to get there. You are the empath.

For a good deal of time during the devalue stage, the co narc will become incredibly angry at times and the number of confrontations would increase. This can last for a good duration. But what often happens is the co narc will bounce back to the love-bombing stage. They will need a certain feed, and they feel going back to the love-bombing stage will get it for them. They will come and say they are sorry and they will be nice again. They will do all those special things again, and this leads to trauma bonding. And sadly, because they are great manipulators, you will fall for it every time.

The victim will pacify the situation by saying, "Okay, the tough time is over and things will get better now. All I have to do now is use logic and things will stay good." And they believe it. It is important to understand these stages are very defined and very distinct. The victim is always trying to get the co narc in a good mood and hopes that they will stay there.

Unfortunately, this love-bombing stage does not last long. You not being as they want you to be is simply unacceptable. They will criticize you to your face and to anyone around you. They will make your life a living hell. They will attack you with rage, often relentless and illogical. It is known that this stage can last for several months. There is no love and no affection, and no matter how hard you try, they are miserable. It is bad.

I do not care how many bouquets of flowers you buy for them or boxes of candy you bring home. You are an evil person and did not get it right. Any favors you do for them or any restaurant you pick, you will not make them happy. And the survivor will take this personally. Very cruel.

This is also showing that they really do not have any love or affection for you. That is the bottom line I wish to make here. Many wish they could have learned the lesson here and left the co narc, but the survivor stays because they are blind. If this is you, run now!

Often, during a disagreement with a normal partner, the person will argue their piece and move on. A co narc will argue and argue and keep it going until you are so exhausted mentally, you cannot see straight. They will argue the same piece with the same claims long after they made their point. They will beat the dead horse just to keep you off balance, just to keep you upset. Upsetting you is a weird but true way of making them happy. They love to see you unhappy. Again, this is the mental abuse we spoke about. This abuse could be much worse than physical abuse because it messes around with your mind.

It is easy to just walk away if you could. If the argument occurs in a house or in the backyard, yes, you can walk away. But if you are driving in a car or in a place where you cannot simply walk away, it can be extremely nerve-racking. The co narc knows this, and they know the strategies that work the best. They know how to get to you, and they will exploit their tactic skillfully when you are the most vulnerable. They are not going to let things go. They will argue to get their fill, but it will never come. Their insecurity comes flowing out, and you are going to hear it.

Not only does the criticism increase over this course of the relationship, but the number of rules will also increase. And the more the bizarre these new rules will become. There will be rules for you but none for them. Whenever you want to make a request for something you wish for them to do or not do, they will not take it seriously. It will go in one ear and out the other. How dare you put borders up on them? But the rules they demand from you will now become law. And if you break the law, you will pay. Yes, you will pay big and you will feel the rage.

In most narcissistic relationships, there will be the love-bombing stage followed by the devalue stage, then when the co narc needs supply again, they will go back to love-bombing again. But understand me here when I tell you that they are in the devalue stage, which is most of the time. Any information you give them or any advice you share with them, they will not believe. The co narc, deep down, hates you so much that no matter what you tell them or any advice you give them, their first response will to be disprove it. They will disagree immediately.

If a coworker, family member, or even a total stranger tells the co narc something, they will believe it without question. When you tell the co narc anything, their defense shields go up, and it will be nonsense. The co narc cannot afford for you to be right and look good. They cannot give you any satisfaction and must crush you and your information. But anything you tell them will not only be the only way they will devalue you but also anything you do.

Any favor you do for them or any chore you complete will simply not be acceptable. There will be something not right with what you did. Again, this can be crushing to the survivor because the survivor needs fill too. A normal amount of fill not insurmountable.

Again, mental and emotional abuse. The survivor will not give up trying to satisfy the co narc, and they will set themselves up again for failure. But on the flip side, should the co narc do a rare favor for the survivor, it better be met with an enthusiastic praise and appreciation. If not, there will be hell to pay.

Now, it is important to remember the co narc has no soul. They are very insecure, so to keep themselves where they want, you become their target. They will control you because they cannot control themselves. They are disappointed with themselves. They do not like who they are. So when you break one of their rules or cause them narcissistic injury, you cannot disappoint them. You stepped out of their bounds. How dare you; so you must pay.

They will find a weakness, either true or not, something you personally shared with them; and they will exploit it. No, they will not find a weakness; they already know the weakness because you trusted them. They had been holding this weakness in a locked box, and they were holding it for just the right time. And they will use it against you at the most advantageous time. If you got a speeding ticket, you would become the worst driver. If you enjoyed an occasional beer or wine, you were a drunk. You will be a slob, an insensitive and incapable jerk. Remember, they are planning the discard well before they do it. So they are setting it up the whole time.

They are now bored of you and wish to start looking for their next victim or their next out, their next fill. They hate you so much, they cannot image it. So they will devalue you. It makes them feel good when you are down, so they try putting you down and will do everything they can to keep you down. It's sick, but take it to the bank. It is true.

They will start to criticize you on everything you say and do. They will do it in front of people and in private. The way you dress, the way you walk, the things you say, and especially anything you do or buy them. They will go out with their friends for dinner and totally smear you. They will tell them inflated stories about nominal things, and yes, they will also come out with straight out lies. They now must destroy you for you being just you and not for being perfect. And they will be hateful and ruthless and will show no mercy, no remorse, and especially no conscience.

They will come home after being with family and friends and start to tell you how all their family and friends can see that you are a horrible person, that your partner is too good for you. How could they put up with you? Again, exaggerated truths and straight out lies.

You will see a change. Oh boy, you will see a change. It will occur in a flash. It will come fast, and it will be hard. There will be no love, no compassion, nor feelings. You will see a distinctive look in their eyes. You will become frustrated. You will feel lonely, and the chances of confrontations will increase. The fighting will start over nothing, and you will now begin to wonder why. You will not even know what you are fighting about.

You will search your soul. You know you did nothing wrong. You have been the same person all along. You did not cheat on them. You did not hit them, nor did you gamble away the house. You are not criticizing them nonstop. You're not picking on them nor devaluing them. But now you are fighting uncontrollably. What changed? You may or may not realize it, but they did not change one iota. They are still the same insecure person. They did not change one bit. But what did change? *You did*. You changed. You stopped being a pushover.

You caused narcissistic damage. You made a stand. You said no. You were not supposed to do that. How dare you hurt their fragile ego? You are the shiny new car, and now, you will not start. You have a flat tire or a crack in the windshield. Your worthless to them. They liked the car, they liked the way they looked in the car, and they liked the way the car drove. But as soon as the car did not do the things they needed, they hated the car. No love, no reason to keep it.

They want another new car just like you. They like the things you did for them. They loved how you looked or what you bought for them. They loved how you made them look. Again, they are an empty soul. How they look is especially important to them. But they never loved you. That bond that you grew with them, they never got with you. You did not make them feel good anymore. Just like they did not get the love bond with the car, they never nor could they ever get that bond with you. Again, you are their possession—nothing more, nothing less. Remember, when they come back—and they will try to come back—they will never change. They cannot.

One point I wish to make here is that you, as the victim of abuse, understand. You understand the pain and misery of a narcissistic relationship. Nobody can explain it. But get together with another survivor, and you immediately will speak the same language.

So what does that mean to this situation? You as a victim now can look at people, and you will be able to identify who is abused by a narcissistic partner and who is not. Not only will you identify one, but you can also understand when they speak. You will feel their pain.

There was a cartoon that explains this clearly. It shows two chalkboards with two people next to each. The first clip shows the chalkboard with many complex mathematical equations written on it, and the caption says, "A narcissist survivor explaining their pain to a non-narcissist survivor." The second clip has 2+2=4. Its captions read, "A narcissist survivor explaining the pain to another narcissist survivor." We understand each other. You are not alone. We all speak the same language.

The devalue/triangular phase can be very painful. But as painful as it is, it does not compare to the discard.

The Discard

Okay, I am not going to sugarcoat this. There is no use beating around the bush. This is like when the doctor tells you, "This will not hurt a bit. You are only going feel a small pinch." Trust me, you are not. This is going to or has hurt big.

If you had a long relationship with a co narc, things are going to appear normal. I say normal not in reference to a normal relationship. I mean normal for your unique relationship. And boom! Just like that, this is going to come out of left field. One day, you are going for walks every evening, thinking everything is fine. The next moment, it is over. Most decisions to discard happens extremely quick.

And the victim will know right away when the discard phase has begun. And I find this is a very important time for the victim to pay attention to, and it is imperative that the victim trusts their instincts. The signs will be very prevalent, very distinctive. And since it will happen quickly, the victim will see a distinct difference in the way the co narc acts.

The difference between the devalue stage and the discard stage is that during the devalue stage, the co narc will be devaluing and triangulating but then will become very warm and loving like a light switch when the co narc needs some fill from the victim. It will be the typical on-and-off situation, just like the black-and-white, good-or-bad, never a gray area kind of living—the only way a co narc knows how to live.

When the discard phase begins, everything will be black, bad, and off. There will be no white, no good, nor any on. Anything that the victim says will not be heard, nor will anything the victim does be seen. It will become a dark and gloomy place. Now this phase can last a considerable amount of time. It will not be a pleasant time nor be anything the victim will enjoy. When this phase starts, the victim must realize it and protect themselves both physically and mentally.

But unfortunately, many times, the victim will not see the signs or more probably simply not believe their own senses. The victim almost always will, at this point, try harder to satisfy the co narc. But this will be like bailing out the *Titanic* with a thimble. Now it is still possible for the cycle to start all over again. The co narc may bounce out of the discard and enter the devalue stage or even back into the love-bombing stage, all depending on how the co narc feels.

Some people who are survivors of narcissistic abuse have experienced the discard stage several times before the actual out-the-door discard happens. That is why, many times, the victim will not believe the co narc will leave. They will try very hard to get the co narc back into the love-bombing stage and get that dose of dopamine. They may believe they could ride out the storm and not take the discard seriously. So when the actual discard occurs, the victim is really in a bad area. The fall is hard, and the pieces are harder to pick up. So I am hoping to educate all the victims out there and teach them how to identify the first discard. When it happens, leave.

What happens to many victims during the discard stage is they will be made the aggressor. They will be made to look like the bad guy. Remember, the co narc is a master and will do anything to not look bad and to look like the victim, especially to people around them. They will treat the victim so badly and so cold, without love, affection, or compassion. Again, this could last a long time, sometimes over a year.

The victim is simply a lonely person looking for attention. The victim sometimes will either become tired and now leave the co narc or will seek attention in the arms of another. If this occurs, the co narc will sit back and point out to all around who will listen to them and will say, "See, I tried so hard at this relationship and they left me," or say, "They cheated on me." They want so bad for the victim to step out of line because it is all about how others see the co narc, and gaining sympathy is power for them.

Why did they discard you? It is very simple. The co narc did not change; they did not change one bit. The stars not aligning is a certain pattern, nor did hell freeze over. It is very simple. They discarded you because, very simply, you changed. You would not play the game anymore. You said no, the word the co narc cannot handle, the word they never want to hear; and now, they hate you.

Yes, they hate you. You no longer fed into their ego. You're not doing what they want you to do. You became a person that they can no longer control, and now they cannot stand you. They never manufactured that love bond with you like other lovers do, so now you are that gorgeous car that just will not start. You are that beautiful dress that they showed off at the last dinner party because it made them look good and everyone marveled at, but now, you have a big stain on you.

You are independent. You are confident, and you radiate it. They needed you to bring them up. You are a person they wish they could be. They sucked off you, and now they realize there is nothing else to suck. Or you will not give any more to them. You may have loved them. You may feel that you needed them, but the truth is they needed you more but they did not love you ever.

This is because the co narc becomes bored with the victim very quickly, or the co narc has found a new supply. Now I do not mean they just decided that they were done with you because, again, they were planning the discard for quite some time, probably most of the relationship. But the actual *we are done* comes quick. They simply do not care what the situation is nor your feelings. They do not care what you are going through nor if they hurt you.

It makes them feel better if they hurt you harder. It gives them the feeling of satisfaction. No matter what, you're yesterday's news. And in most cases, and this is what is very hard as a victim, there is no closure. There is no *I am leaving because X, Y, Z*. They do not care whether the victim is dedicated to dealing with a different situation like taking care of an ailing parent or dealing with a business condition. They do not care. Believe it or not, they will purposely choose when things like this are going on because they have a sick affliction of feeling good when you are hurting. They will often choose this time to hurt the victim.

Then the victim is left there as always—confused and off balance. But I wish to emphasize again that this was going to happen. It was in the planning stages for a long time. It was part of their plan. There was nothing the victim could have done to avoid this or change it, and the co narc simply does not care. So it is most important to understand: Do not blame yourself. You should compliment yourself for putting up with the co narc for as long as you did and now, most of all, get on your knees and thank God they left.

They did you a favor, a big favor. Even at first, the victim will not comprehend it. The victim may replay scenarios in their head of incidents that happened in the past and start making excuses for the co narc. They may tell themselves, *Had I only done this different or done that in a better manner.* Forget it. It will not help.

After the discard, this could be a very stressful time for the victim. They feel all the emotions I mentioned at the beginning of this book. But as soon as the victim takes some time to understand who they were dealing with and what they were dealing with, they go out and get some help. The pain and suffering will subside. It will truly never go away, but it will lessen.

This is hard mentally and emotionally for the victim because it is not a mutual or usual breakup. During a usual breakup, both parties usually move apart, and the feelings are mutual. Maybe some infidelity, maybe a good deal of fighting, and both persons agree it is time to move on. But just like the entire relationship with the co narc, they attack emotionally. They work against you mentally, and they will catch you off guard. It is on purpose and all part of the plan. And again, those scars that do not show run the deepest, and they take the longest to heal.

After the discard has been decided, the devaluing and triangulation will increase at this point to pinnacle levels; and there will be absolutely no love, attention, or affection—zero. They will amp up the contempt and hatred they have for you now. But this is where you need to be careful. This is where you need to listen very carefully to the words they are saying. The co narc is staying and have not moved on for one reason and one reason only—the co narc is not done sucking everything they can off you before they throw you to the curb.

You still have some worth to them or have unfinished business with the victim. They still need you and can get one more ounce out of you. You, being the empath, will put on the good-guy cap; and you will be trying to keep things together, thinking this is just another temper tantrum. The co narc is taking because they have had them before and this will all subside in some time, but the co narc is planning their escape and is quietly setting it up.

They will be saving or hiding money; setting up bank accounts; and gaining information about bank information, retirement funds, and insurance. They will also be setting up the people around you. Triangulation will be in overdrive at this point, and the co narc may start to exhibit physical rage. You will see the flying monkeys and be hearing the sad things being told about you. Most of these things will be false or misleading.

The discard is designed to crush you. It is supposed to paralyze you. It is so you cannot function without them. They do not want you to succeed, do better, or be happy without them especially with someone new. They always had to be the center of your attention. They had to mold you to the way they wanted you. You are not to be able to live without them.

The co narc will choose a time to discard you when you are the most vulnerable and the weakest. They will simply have no sympathy, no remorse, nor empathy. They are incapable to exhibit these traits. Trust me when I tell you that. The person you thought were so kind and nice, who put on such a fake persona especially when others were around, will surprise you with how cruel and mean they can be. The creature you thought would only appear in horror movies is now standing in your living room.

I know this hurts the victim the greatest. This is where most of the pain the victim will receive will be. They will be so surprised and taken aback, they now will understand that they did not mean anything to this person. What they will understand after they do some research was that they never did. They never meant anything to them. They were just that object that fed their fill. They built that bond in their head like most people who fall in love. They cared so much for this person. Yes, it will hurt. The victim may begin to have trust issues here.

When the co narc enters the discard phase, it is over. Put a fork in it. Do not think for one minute that they were playing or in just another wild, crazy mood or anything else. It is over. You cannot fix it. You cannot change their minds, so do not even try. They are leaving, they have already lined up their next victim or next supply, and you are already the cowboy in black.

Why do some discards last so long? Because again, the victim is trying to hold things together and the co narc is still sucking everything they can. They may coddle the co narc or do unusually nice things to try to calm down the co narc. And the co narc may and will take advantage of this vulnerability of the victim. They will exploit the victim at this point, so do not play the fool.

The co narc, at this point, will be going out and either find or look for the next supply. But when the co narc leaves the victim, they are overconfident most of the time. They come off believing they are invincible. They just took total advantage of the victim. You were totally fooled and under total control of the co narc. They go out believing they can do this not only to their new supply but also to family and friends.

Remember, you cannot hide the crazy for long. And in many cases, the co narc will hook up with another narcissist. This will lead to a struggle for control. Nor is the empath and both are looking for fill. No matter who the co narc takes as their next supply, they will believe the new supply will play the game just like the survivor did.

This can be very eye-opening to the co narc or, put in another way, a big dose of reality. They will try to love bomb, gaslight, and do everything they can to suck the new supply in. But again, it is just a matter of time before the new supply will put the black cowboy suit on and the co narc will start the devaluation stage. It will happen. Call your bookie and place the bet. So predictable.

Some couples may even seek professional or spiritual help. I will not say that professional counseling cannot help, but I will. Do not waste your time, energy, or money. Look, I have nothing against marriage counseling nor other psychological help to help people find happiness and understanding. I recommend the survivor get some help for themselves for dealing with the abuse from a co narc. But for any of these sciences to help, the person or persons seeking help must be willing to change.

The patient must listen and learn, then make changes. The co narc may wish to go and the victim may agree and go, but the co narc is not and does not nor is capable of changing. The co narc will blame you for everything. They want to look like the kind, sweet person trying so hard to keep things together and make you look like a totally selfish, self-centered loser. They also will, in their own head, make excuses as to why they did the things they did to you and why they treated you so poorly.

Remember, they are the expert in manipulation. They are focused like a laser; and you are reeling, confused, and disoriented. In this case, counseling will not work and this cannot be overstated simply because the co narc will not and cannot change. They will never self-reflect, admit guilt, nor think that they have done any wrongdoing. You will bear the blame for everything. You were the problem. You needed to change, and the co narc will play the victim, a part they do so well.

So trust me; do not even waste your time. They will also project many of their own insecurities onto you. Gaslighting these insecurities at you, you will become confused and off balance again and start soul-searching, trying to put things together. Maybe even believe them. But deep down inside, you know the truth. So the important thing here is trust your heart.

Remember, they are the one that is so upset. They are the one that is off. Any advice the counselor may give them, they will not accept it, nor will they self-reflect. They cannot be wrong; it's you. Narcissists cannot be cured, so face reality. If you were discarded, thank God.

My point is, if you believe you are being discarded, you are being discarded. So open your eyes and get educated and protect yourself. They will show no remorse nor empathy. Do not be blind. Fight back. The co narc's worst fear at this point is that you will discard them first, that you will shut them out. Do not be a fool. Beat them to it.

But even after the discard and they have moved on and you are there picking up the pieces, the co narc is not done with you and will keep their eyes on you. They never will fully be done with you because they know you were a useful source of supply and an honorable person. They will keep in touch with you because they just want to keep the connection open because they may need you again, and they will try to keep the tabs on you to make sure or at least hope you're not doing better without them. But trust me, the best defense and the most effective way to heal from your time with this person is to go no contact. This is highly and a mostly effective weapon. It may not be easy, but it is effective if you do it right.

Hoovering

There are many terms that get thrown around in this topic of narcissistic abuse. Hoovering is a term which happens mostly after the co narc discarded you and both you and they have moved on, but basically, the co narc will hoover anytime that they will feel their control over the victim is lost or wavering. The co narc will try to get the victim to either come back to them or at least try to get them under control again.

They want their power back, they want their total control again, and they want the good thing that they had before. Remember, control is a must for the co narc. Hoovering usually occurs after some time after the discard and often after the victim went no contact. The co narc will also hoover after they failed in a new relationship and they are feeling vulnerable, and they realize they had a good thing before.

Will the co narc hoover you? I will say an almost definite yes and would place a good bet on it. Since you are reading this, trying to figure out what happened and why, it means you were hurt; and most of all, you cared. And the biggest and hardest hurt comes from people you are the closest to, the people you mostly care for, the people you least expect it from. So your heart was in the relationship, which means you were a good supply of fill, or else the co narc would have move on much earlier.

You, for a good period, gave that fill to the co narc. You loved them and tried hard to put up with their madness. The co narc will try to find that fill with other sources, and they will hold your fill as the standard and the new supply may not measure up. Almost always, the new source will not measure up to you so they will fall short and the new relationship will crumble. The co narc will desire that fill you gave them, so eventually, they will come looking for the fill you had. Not guaranteed but a good bet.

It may be a simple text message at first or a simple reach out on social media. They will just dip their toe in the water to see where they stand. It is very important here to know that any reply to the co narc will be taken as a sign that you can still give them fill, and most of all, they can control again.

Another reason they may hoover you is that they may see you happy with a new partner, and this is harmful to their fragile ego. It is something that they do not want, and they must fix that. The co narc, who so desperately needs supply and knows where they receive good supply before in your relationship, will try to destroy your happiness. Remember, they not only want you not to do as well as them but they also must destroy you. They do not care at all about you or your feelings or your well-being. Hoovering can occur after a week or sometimes after several decades, so stay on your toes.

Hoovering often works for the co narc because the victim believes the co narc can or will change. Also, trauma bonding will become a factor in the situation. Unfortunately, the victim often forgets a good deal of all the horrible treatment at the hands of the co narc that happened before and the disappointing times with the co narc.

They often remember the happy times and the times the dopamine in their brains was plentiful. And let us not forget that the co narc knows exactly how to gaslight and manipulate the victim better than anyone else. They did it before. They practiced it, and they will turn up the heat and put the gaslighting program into overdrive. Unfortunately, they may catch the victim at a time when the victim was vulnerable in their life and the victim wants to believe the co narc when they say they will change or that things are different now.

The co narc may even admit to some of the complaints that the victim may have had when they were together, and they will promise that they will do better and will act proper. The co narc may even try to use all kinds of different tactics, such as love bombing and the all popular guilt bombing. Remember, the co narc is a master at portraying themselves as the victim and you as the aggressor, and they can turn the tables rather quickly and make the real victim believe they were part of the problem if not the entire problem with the relationship.

Yes, welcome back to gaslighting. You would not be here if you were not originally susceptible to the co narc and their tactics. And often, empaths who always want to help others and never want to see others in pain is a victim again. Another technique they can try is they will play hopeless. They will tell the victim that they have moved on but they are nothing without the victim. They understand what the victim did for them and how they did not appreciate them. But the victim should listen to that little voice in their head. That little voice should come over loud and clear like a bullhorn. Unfortunately, sometimes they do not.

The victim may, now that they have researched the topic of narcissism or went and sought professional help, feel emboldened and think that they are able to handle the co narc and be prepared to all their old tricks.

They believe they will be able to see the early the signs of trouble, and they will have their shields up. They can fight back with a vengeance. Unfortunately, the co narc will easily retract those shields and the victim will let their guard down. And it may be a wonderful experience in the new beginning, just like it was when the relationship started or when the last hoovering occurred several times before.

But just like a leopard does not change his spots, nor does a narcissist change their attitude. Unfortunately, the co narc will resort to their old tendencies. But their tools will now be sharper than they were before. They will cut deeper and create more painful scars. So do not fall for the hoover.

But a really important point that I would like to make here is that the co narc does not want you back. They do not want the person you are; they do not want the bond that you once had with them. They want to suck off you again. They want what you could give them. The selfishness comes out, and they do not care if they hurt you. And again, it is guaranteed to fail. Guaranteed!

And when it does, because you had an emotional connection rekindle and they did not, you will be left there picking up the pieces of your heart again. They will move on to the next thing that will give them the fill, and you will be there left in the dark. They will feel no remorse or guilt whatsoever. So if you educated yourself correctly, you would protect yourself and reject the hoover. They did it to you before probably many times, so learn from it.

Sometimes, hoovering could also occur during the devalue or the discard stages of the relationship. In these stages, it is because the co narc is losing control or feels they need something from the victim. They may feel the victim is moving away from or is not paying enough attention to them or anytime the co narc feels they are losing control.

So the first thing they will do is try to love bomb the victim. They already know what makes you tick, and again, they will try to control you again. The cycle of love bombing, devaluing, discarding to hoovering can last a long time. Sometimes, for as long as thirty years. And it is important to point out they the order will occur not in any predictable order. This keeps most unhealthy narcissistic relationship going.

The victim knows the relationship is not normal. They know there is a problem, but they really love the co narc. Unfortunately, they do not know they are a victim. The co narc will devalue; and this could last for a while, then hoover back to love bombing stage, back to the devalue stage, and may reach the discard stage, hoovering back to the love bombing. That is why when the co narc finally gets to the final discard stage and discards the victim, this will catch the victim off guard because the victim was so used to the hoovering to commence and was waiting for the hoovering back to the love-bombing stage.

This is one reason why it can be difficult for the victim to move on because it is a big surprise. It catches the victim off guard, and while they are stunned, the co narc is focused like a laser. And it is usually why the co narc will appear to do better because it will appear they are steady and strong and you are an insecure stiff.

Gaslighting

As we stated before, a narcissist is excellent at manipulation and dilution. They become incredibly good at getting what they want. They will make you believe things differently from want you know are the truth. They will gaslight you into believing things that play well in their head but not in reality.

Gaslighting is a term which means the person speaking is tricking the person listening into believing something not true or is bending the truth. It is a form of straight out lying; but it is even more devious than just that because it works on a psychological, mental, and emotional level. The speaker is not just lying to the victim; they are trying to control the victim psychologically and mentally. If the victim is being controlled, then they are easier to control and better to provide feed to the abuser or co narc. This is very scary and devious.

The term gaslighting comes from an old story where a man was trying to convince his wife that she was crazy even though she was totally sane. He did this because his wife loved him and trusted him, and the husband did this by doing different devious things around the home, then he would convince her that she was wrong. He would hide and move things around the house and then tell his wife that she was losing her mind. He would triangulate and tell other people who felt separate ways about her.

The setting occurs from a time when electric lighting was limited, so most of the lighting in the home was powered by natural gas. One of the devious things the husband would do is go into the family attic and turn on all the lights up there, and this would cause the rest of the lights in the rest of the home to dim due to the loss of pressure of gas. And as you can guess, when the wife would say something about the lighting in the home dimming, the husband would tell her she is simply not seeing what she knew was correct.

He not only lied to her, but he also psychologically and mentally deceived her. He dominated her; he had total control of her and the way she thought. She was not unbalanced. This was unfair to her. She was not free to be the person she wanted to be. She became dependent on him. And what most find troubling about this is she trusted him.

The co narc knows the truth, but they will gaslight into convincing you something that you know is not correct. The co narc will deceive you and make you believe you're crazy when you really know the truth. They will bend the truth and straight out lie. They will tell you that you are incorrect and make you believe something totally obscure. And like the woman in the story, you trusted and loved them.

You have the simple knowledge of believing the co narc would not lie to you. Again, when you are confused and off-kilter, you are easily controlled and they are allowed to get away with anything. And that is where they want you. As we said before, when the question was asked if a co narc is aware of what they are doing and the damage that they are doing, the answer is an emphatic yes.

They know exactly what they are doing. They are aware of the damage they are causing. But they are not able to comprehend the problem they are causing, and more importantly, they do not care. But this is all part of their survival. They will maintain the lie for their own benefit. If you are gaslighted, you are being controlled. You are a pawn in the co narc's scheme. Manipulation, deception, and control are critical for their survival. It is something that they had become incredibly good at.

Remember, they do not care about the survivor. They do not care about the damage they are causing. The only thing they care about is their own ego and control. What is in it for them? This is where the co narc can be extremely dangerous. This is where they can cause severe damage to the survivor. And this is simply unfair for the survivor.

Just as we said before, the survivor is already walking on eggshells and afraid to do anything that might tip the co narc off. Now, they do not know which way is up. The things they believed are correct are now off. The things that they believe is off is now not only correct but now the norm. The survivor is constantly being kept on the defensive and off balance.

One way the co narc will gaslight you are that they will devalue you to your family and friends. They will tell them manipulating stories about you, stories that may or may not be true, stories that are exaggerated. It may have some truth to it, but the new story will have twisted parts to favor the co narc's narrative. At that point, they will come home to you and tell you your family and friends were telling them how horrible you are, bending the truth in the opposite way to make their story.

Again, of course, they know what they are doing. So, why do they do it? To make themselves look better, to try to keep you in line, to make themselves feel better, to gain sympathy from unfamiliar souls, and to set you up for the discard. And most of all, they stay superior to you.

Yes, they were planning the discard from early in the relationship. Also, they do not wish for you to gain the spotlight. They want the spotlight only on them. You cannot and must not outshine them. They are already jealous of you, and they must be in control. Remember, they know eventually when they grow tired of you and/ or you cannot fill that huge ego of theirs, they are going to discard you. So they need to set it up.

Again, what they look like to other people and how they appear is especially important. They look like a sweet and empathetic person if they put up with a person like you. They tried so hard to make things work. They tried so hard and did everything possible while you were so unbearable and unwilling to try when, in the real world, you deserve a medal dealing and putting up with them.

Gaslighting not only occurs on the momentary timeline. It also could last for many years, just constantly snowballing, changing course as it rolls down the hill, and gaining in size and speed to suit the co narc's needs. This is normal to the co narc, and unfortunately, it will become normal for you.

Another way the co narc will gaslight their victims is when you catch them in a lie or witness them doing something that is questionable or is simply not correct. Instead of them listening and self-reflecting, they will change their story or they will automatically go on the offensive and bring up things you did in the past.

An example of this is if the co narc spent a good some of money on something questionable and you confront them on this. They will immediately turn the table and attack you on something you bought in the past that they thought was questionable. Or they will find a way to blame you for why they did what they did. You were the reason they did what they did. They are never wrong; they will never self-reflect.

In many cases, the co narc will dig in their heels and not give any quarter. So now, the survivor feels that it is just not worth the fight, so either ignore it or just give up, the wrong thing to do. They will just expand the co narc's boundaries, diminish yours, and become more emboldened in their lies and deception.

Trauma Bonding

During a relationship with a co narc, one can fall into a condition called trauma bonding. Trauma bombing can become a very powerful and an obsessive tactic used by the co narc against the victim or something that unfortunately happens in a narcissistic relationship, even though the victim does not even know that they are being trauma bonded nor do they consciously know that this is happening.

I believe the co narc does not even know why trauma bonding works at all. The co narc is subconsciously behaving in a way that keeps the victim trapped. Trauma bonding is a term used when the victim becomes addicted to the abuse or simply does not know the difference between crazy living given by the co narc and normal living. What happens is that the victim becomes addicted to the abuse and they lose sight of reality. They simply lose the path of what is happiness and what is a vile way of living or simply the way they wish to live.

They become obsessed with pleasing the co narc or at least not pissing them off. As sick as this is true, the victim will become addicted to the abuse dealt by the co narc. Many victims will deal with the poor treatment because they are afraid of even more severe circumstances, or they are such empaths that they keep trying to not hurt the co narc. They are afraid of the unknown, or they have forgotten what normal is. But mostly, the victim believes the co narc will change and become happy. Not going to happen.

Trauma bonding works because of chemicals in the victim's brain. When something good or desirable occurs, they often feel guilty to the co narc or unworthy of such a good behavior. Many times, trauma bonding takes effect so slowly during the relationship that it happens undetected. The victim starts to believe that this treatment is normal behavior and will become expecting the poor treatment, or they will put up with the co narc's treatment because they know when the poor treatment ends, the good or normal behavior feels like a reward.

A familiar term is that the bar is set low. The victim has become infected with tunnel vision. That means the victim becomes so compelled and obsessed with not upsetting the co narc, they are only focused on making sure the co narc stays happy. It often becomes a challenge. But as always, the co narc will find something to be unhappy about. They love being unhappy, and more importantly, they love making others unhappy. This again is simply unfair to the victim because they are not being the person who they are or who they want to be. They are very uncomfortable and off balance. The victim's whole life is now becoming totally controlled. They become totally submissive, and they become all too compelled to fit this narrative.

During the times that the abuser is inflicting their pain, the victim now becomes stressed and tense, and as a natural defense, the body will secrete different hormones such as cortisol into their bloodstream to deal with the higher stress levels brought on by the abuse. And some of these hormones are known to cause several medical problems in the body, no less than leading to weight gain, headaches, and digestive problems, just to name the few. So being in a narcissistic relationship is both unhealthy physically and mentally.

This part of the relationship is the hardest to move on from. As I have joined several support groups, the most common question is, Should I take my narcissist back because they say they are sorry and they will change? We will address this question in a later chapter. But the answer is always without a doubt no!

The best way to address this disease is it is like quitting smoking, drinking, or gambling. All these addictions are bad for you, but people still do them. The chemicals in your brain are looking to align to find that one point to bring you happiness. Unfortunately, all these bad habits, including trauma bonding, all occur in the same part of the brain. So a gambler knows he should stop gambling, a drinker knows he needs to stop drinking, a smoker knows they need to stop smoking, and a victim of a co narc knows they need to get rid of the co narc. But like all those other diseases, this is a bad habit that is tough to break.

Once discarded, as I said before, the victim will need to find out who they are. They are no longer focused on pleasing the co narc. They will need some time to figure out how to please themselves. They will need to find out what is reality again. They will need to find out which way was up. They now need to find out how to make themselves happy instead of not making their partner unhappy. This can become a very challenging thing. But over time, it will happen.

Being gaslighted and trauma bonded for so many years will obscure their ideas of reality. And when they enter a new relationship, they mentally need to change their perspective on many levels, not only making their partner happy but also how to make themselves happy. Learning that they can say no. It takes some time before they realize the truth again. They need to take it slowly, not worry, and live life.

One of the things that will be very amazing is how most relationships are easy to be in. You will not be tied down from what you could say, when you could say it, and how you acted, always looking for what you needed to do when you needed to do it. You are now able to do things when and where you want. You could be you again and not worry about making someone angry, not pissing someone off, or keeping a keen eye on your co narc partner.

Not worrying when that car door closes or when the company went home and you are alone with your new partner, there will be calmness and peaceful talk, not a barrage of insults and the unnecessary needing to explain yourself because of something you said or did. Now, nothing you did was wrong. Nothing you said was out of line, and most importantly you were you at the event. No more walking on eggshells, and you will become the person you wanted to be and who you were born to be. And most importantly, everyone around you will see it. They will see that person with confidence again. You will become so comfortable again, being the person you know. And many people will tell you that they have never seen you be so happy for a long time.

Sometimes, you will reflect about the tough times and all the craziness that you had endured, and you will see how obscure and unhealthy the relationship was. You easily will see the difference now and unfortunately cannot understand why you were so blind before. Again, happiness is the key. And you will never want to go back. But unfortunately, if the co narc wants to come back, it is very difficult to say no.

Many times, trauma bonding will be compared to the Stockholm syndrome. The Stockholm syndrome comes from an incident in the 1970s when the kidnappees became sympathetic to the cause of the kidnappers and were helping the kidnappers against the authorities.

The victim of narcissistic abuse will often have so much sympathy with the co narc that they will often acerbate the treatment they receive from the co narc. They will defend the co narc, and they will not listen to anyone who is trying to help the victim against the co narc. As crazy as that sounds, it is true. Remember, nothing about any of the treatment of the victim is normal. It is all a twisted and tangled situation with no sense of normalcy.

Many victims who are trauma bonded may also have a medical condition come into play which will keep them under the co narc's control. There have been studies which indicates that different amounts of dopamine in the brain and the variable levels during various parts of the relationship.

In a stable relationship, where things are more predictable and without an incredible amount of tension, the amounts of dopamine secretion are stable. There is no big swing in levels of dopamine in the brain when different incidents occur. But it has been found that in a trauma-bonded situation, there is a significant amount of dopamine level changes in the brain. When the victim is under stressful situations, or for many being around a co narc most of the time, it has been discovered that the amount of dopamine in their rain, becomes secreted at a low level.

These low levels often cause stress and anxiety and other mental and emotional destress. The victim will learn how to deal with or just suffer with this of level of trauma. But unfortunately, victims become adjusted and used to these unusually low levels. What happens next is when something desirable happens with the co narc. When the co narc is happy and things are going in a positive direction, it has been found that the levels of dopamine secreted into the brain skyrockets to extremely prominent levels, abnormally prominent levels. The victim feels this high; it gives them a sense of well-being.

This differential of unusually low levels of dopamine to an incredibly overwhelming amount is an incredible change to the victim's emotional and mental senses. This change in levels of dopamine in the brain is what the victim strives for—to get that high. They will put up with the tough times because they become adjusted to the low levels of dopamine, and they crave the differential of dopamine in the brain. Like a person hooked on drugs who gets their hit or when a gambler is on a winning streak, the victim becomes an addict. That is why it is often very difficult to break the trauma bonding.

Unfortunately, many times, the victim will look for other avenues to get to that high that they are not receiving at home. Alcohol, drugs, sex, and/or gambling often become the substitutes for the victim. These outs will increase the levels of dopamine but only temporarily, and as you can see, other bad side effects come into play here that simply do not help the situation, often making things worse.

And unfortunately, this will play into the hands of the co narc. Now, because the victim will seek outside sources to satisfy basic human needs, the co narc will use this as ammunition against the victim. Again, triangulation at its finest. This is the silent problem. It now will show the victim in a poor light and the co narc as the victim, a win for the co narc, a problem that they caused but makes the victim look bad. And this is where the co narc wants to be—shown as the victim when we all know that is simply not the case. It can become frustrating for the real victim, adding to the mental abuse. It becomes so unfair.

I often use the analogy to help explain this scenario. In a football game, it is not the first player who throws the first punch who receives the penalty; it is the player who reacts and throws the second punch that all the referees catch. And out come all the yellow flags, and it is he who will receive the penalty. But in today's live football, there is instant replay where the truth always come out. The players cannot hide.

In a narcissistic relationship, this is not so, and it becomes very frustrating for the victim, the real victim, not the one that the co narc wants you to believe. They know exactly what they are doing and when to do it. They know when they could get away with things and when they need to act appropriately. This solves the question, does the co narc know if they are being deceitful and dishonest? That answer is a definite yes.

This makes the co narc happy, who has already decided that it was just a matter of time before the discard was going to happen, and it will give the co narc something against the victim, showing anyone who will listen that they were the good one in the relationship. And the victim, having cheated on them or used drugs or became a drunk, was the bad one; and this will bring sympathy for the co narc.

Speaking the Language

One point I would like to bring out here and make very clear. When a victim of narcissistic abuse tries to explain this situation to someone who is unfamiliar with this type of mental disorder or has never experienced this type of abuse before in their life, it is near impossible for the listener to understand. They may think you are exaggerating or making stuff up, or they do not understand the pain and suffering.

But please understand that victims are not alone. You are not the only person fighting this fight. The number of co narc survivors is high and unfortunately getting higher. If you set out and seek help—and there are many avenues in which you can do this—it will be very eye-opening and satisfying by talking to someone who is knowledgeable in this area. By speaking to someone who understands narcissism, narcissistic abuse, or is a survivor of narcissistic abuse because they understand.

They get it. They will automatically interact with you and give you support and reinforcement. They will tell you of their own struggles with this disease. This will become very relieving and will bring some sanity to the victim. Remember, all co narcs act the same way. The tactics that they use, all the abuse they commit, is uncannily similar. And as soon as the victim realizes this, the healing can commence. And victims deserve to be heard.

Another avenue the victim may seek to escape the craziness is in the arms of another. Many times, when the co narc is abusing its victim for a good deal of time, the victim just wants someone who listen to them, someone who is just nice to them. Or someone not just nice to them but actually paid some attention to the victim. The victim was just looking for some realm of normalcy, somebody from work or somebody they may know from the gym. Not that this is ethically correct, nor am I condoning this behavior.

It is often looked down upon by many, but it happens. And who are we to judge? Nobody knows the pain and hurt a survivor had endured. But should this get back to the co narc, this will cause severe narcissistic injury to them and serious injury to the victim. The co narc will turn the tables and portray themselves as the poor soul.

Baiting

It is important to restate the co narc must be in control. *Always*. This is where they feel the most comfortable, and they will do anything to get there and most importantly maintain it. Many times, when the co narc loses control or they believe they are about to lose control, they will often resort to baiting to regain control.

The co narc will first try the usual tactics—love bombing, devaluation, triangulation, flying monkeys—to put the victim back into line. But for one reason or another reason, these tactics are not working and the victim is not following or acting the way the co narc expects. The victim is not playing the usual game. So now, the co narc will switch gears and turn up the heat and will start baiting.

Baiting is when the co narc often attacks the victim with something the co narc knows will get under the victim's skin or something that the victim is insecure or sensitive about. The co narc will start a fight or confrontation for no realm or reason. The victim usually does not see it coming and almost always will catch the them off guard, not just off guard but at a time when the victim is not ready or in a position to handle the attack. It will be during a party or a gathering when family and friends are present, and it is the last thing the survivor is expecting.

The co narc will be rude or vicious about a topic that the co narc knows will normally get the victim upset. Many times, the victim will get upset, rattled, and worked up. The victim then may become irate, aggravated, and will fight back. Unfortunately, the victim will often, because of bottled-up anger, react in an uncharacteristic way.

Earlier, I made the analogy about the football player who receives the penalty not being the first player to throw the punch but the player who reacts and strikes back. Usually, the strike back is stronger and more aggressive. Well, after the co narc ignites the fuse, it is normal for the victim to get worked up and become unhinged. The co narc will now step back and act with the attitude, *Hey, look at you. You are all upset. You are overreacting. And I'm just standing here calm, cool, and collected. So you must be crazy. You're the one with the problem.*

They will especially do this when you are around others and when they have an audience. They will strike in covertly where nobody can witness, then will then gain the attention of an audience. The co narc often will not only light the fuse, but if the reaction is not as strong or intense as the co narc anticipates, the co narc will throw a little gasoline on the smolders. The co narc will prick and probe to get the reaction they want.

This is gaslighting and triangulation on steroids. The co narc is gaslighting the people around you. They are triangulating to show the victim as the problem, and let us not forget they are looking for attention and sympathy from those same people. Many times, their own flying monkeys will be present, and this will only strengthen their argument of how a horrible person you are.

Baiting is a powerful tool the co narc will use to regain the control. The co narc loves a fight because it puts them in the driver's seat and gives them the power they want and the attention they seek. And because the co narc thrives on chaos, it keeps the victim off balance. To reiterate, the victim is unprepared for the fight and the co narc is focused like a laser. The victim is on an uneven playing field. And most importantly, misery loves company and the co narc is not a happy person. So to see the victim upset, well, that just makes their day.

The point here is the co narc will fight when it is advantageous to them. The co narc will pick and choose their fights and where and when. It is all about how they look.

When the Narcissist Finds Out You Have Figured Them Out or You Are on to Them

This is a place where the co narc does not what to be. This will make them feel extremely uncomfortable, and it will be like cornering an injured animal. You will not know how they might react or what they will do. It is especially important how the co narc appears to others, and they cannot self-evaluate their actions or behaviors. But it is all a show. Remember, the co narc is a shallow person and does not have deep ties. They are only superficial, and they cannot self-reflect.

And if others do not view the co narc in a positive manner, the co narc will panic. And if you attack them with this or cause narcissistic injury, the co narc can react with rage. Remember, they cannot control their emotions because they simply do not understand them. They are not used to not being in control. It is insulting to them. This rage can come out. It will be extreme, and you will be the target.

They will try to get you to react in the way they knew you did before. If you get angry, you are not in control; they are. But if you do not react in the out-of-control way, this will make them unbalanced and put you in the driver seat. They now are in grounds unfamiliar to them. You are now the one focused, and they will often act out.

So keep the control and keep calm; they want that reaction from you. They want to fight. As crazy as it seems, seeing you upset brings joy or satisfaction to them. They want your attention, your total attention, and even bad attention is good attention.

They will also try to use techniques that worked before to keep them in charge, but now, they will ramp those techniques up to a higher intense level to make a more damaging impact on you. They may often resort to triangulation or devaluation. They will try to get to people around you and start to smear you again and make them believe things about you that simply is not true. They will try to get the flying monkeys around you again and let them loose on you. Now that you understand about who you are dealing with, you have done the research, you know how they think and how they act, and you know you were and are not the problem, you can become very comfortable dealing with the co narc; and it can be very damaging to them.

You now have confidence; you have the upper hand and you're educated. The co narc may try to resort to the things that worked on you before. They probably will try to love bomb you again. They will open the old playbook, and they will pick the offensive plays that worked the best before.

If that does not work, they may try going on the offensive and bring out things you have done wrong in the past. They know exactly what buttons to push and which levers to pull and put salt on the wound the quickest. They can, at this point, react with insults, baiting, or projectionism. Which way they go is the way they believe will work the best. But trust me, they do not like being here; it makes them uncomfortable.

This is also a bruise to their already fragile ego. They will do anything to protect that fragile house of playing cards, and they will do anything to keep it from being knocked down. So tread lightly, but now, you will be ready or at least now you will know what you're dealing with and what to expect. But most of all, remember that they cannot hide the crazy forever. The truth always comes out.

Being Able to Identify and Help Other Victims

During the healing process, after doing research and learning about narcissistic abuse, a survivor speaking with people like themselves will be able to start to help other survivors. This can not only become quite satisfying, but it also becomes a two-way healing process because they are helping other people in trouble. It will also help the victim repair or straighten out some emotions that is unsettling in their own head, some old situations that may still be troubling to them.

This can also keep the victim in line and keep themselves from falling back into their co narc's grasp. What I mean is after a discard, whether the co narc discarded the victim or the victim left the co narc, many times, the co narc will try to hoover either to come back to the victim or just keep the victim on a leash and under their control.

The victim may give advice to another survivor to stay no contact or go gray rock. Now that they have given this advice to another person, they are more likely to keep themselves disciplined. Their co narc may try to hoover them or may try to con the victim to take them back. Now, they are more likely to keep to their guns and do the right thing and not fall victim to their poor past.

Over time, a victim of narcissism will be able to identify other victims of narcissism without even having that person admit it. Just like how a bulimic person can walk into a room of people whom they have never met before and be able to point out other people who are bulimic. Or how women who are the victims of physical abuse can identify other women who not only are abused but also women who are not abused. They may not know how they do it or what the signs are, but they can. And victims of narcissism can do this also. They see the signs and right away have empathy. They get it. They can automatically speak with the new person and speak that unique language of narcissist abuse. And again, their stories and tales will be surprisingly similar.

When the Co Narc Gets Caught in a Lie

During your relationship with the co narc, there will be an incredible amount manipulation, distortions of the truth, deception, and outright lies. They will, because they are masters of storytelling and deflection, be able to protect themselves from most accusations, both true and untrue. All narcissists lie; yes, that is a fact. They must. It is part of who they are, and that is the only way they could put on the fake façade which makes them and keeps them safe, the only way they can protect themselves from the outside world.

It is a valuable weapon which protects them from something which may expose themselves as someone other than the perfect person they may think they are or, more importantly, the way everyone else sees them. This becomes a part of their survival. They will do anything to keep anyone away from that fragile house of cards they must protect from being knocked down.

But remember, the co narcs will often show their hand by projectionism. This is a major weakness of the co narc, and the survivor must keep their eyes and ears open and observe what the co narc is saying. It is important to see the whole picture, not just the words that are coming out of their mouth but all the other neon signs they are displaying.

A good analogy here is to picture a bank. A normal person is like a bank. The bank takes in and hands out money, and with the extra money that it takes in, it puts it into the safe. The safe can hold a good deal of money so that if a patron comes to the bank and wants to take out a good sum of cash, the bank can just go into the vault and take it from the vast amounts of savings that it took in. That is how a normal person will handle a small setback or criticism. They just go into who they are and the vast piles of who they are and they can handle most setbacks. The co narc sees this in their victim and wishes they could do this. They envy the victim's ability to just shrug off setbacks and move on.

But a co narc does not have the benefit of having a safe. They do not have the ability to put money or, in their case, confidence into their own vault. Any compliment or self-confidence that they may have received simply is lost. They must depend on a constant supply of deposits from patrons. That supply must be constant and not be interrupted.

But let us say the bank just opened. There was no money in the bank, and the first patron just walked up to the teller window wanted to withdraw ten thousand dollars. This is just like the victim going up to the co narc and telling them they just saw them cheating on them, or they just spent too much money, or confronting them with any other setback. Just like the bank, the co narc must default. They cannot make the payment, so they panic. Just like the bank, they will first try to say, "You really do not want the money now," or say, "You never deposited the money here."

They will often project their own shortcomings and misdeeds onto their victims. Since they always need the feed from others, most of the time, the feed from one person is simply not enough. They need multiple sources of ego stuffing. So many times, they will seek the desire from other sources. They will because they are so shallow and believe they could never be wrong. They will think about that same deed that they committed against the victim and realize that if the victim committed those same deeds against them, it would be devastating to their fragile ego. Remember, the world rotates around the co narc.

So they will often accuse the victim of committing these deeds against them, but the accusations will be hollow. If the co narc, let's say, cheats on the victim, then the co narc will know this is wrong and they will think about this. They know this will make them look bad in the eyes of people around them. This would be, in the boundaries of the co narc, unacceptable and straight out harmful to their ego.

So they will often accuse the victim of committing the very bad deeds they have committed. They will straight come out and say, "I just know you are cheating on me," even though the victim has done nothing to give any suspicion or has done nothing for this accusation. But sometimes, the clues are not so obvious. So the victim needs to look very carefully into the behavior of the co narc.

Watch the actions of the co narc and view the sudden and or hidden signs. If the co narc starts looking into your phone, that may be a sign they have been texting things they do not want you to see or they have contacts that they do not want you to know of. If they are suddenly looking through your car, the signs could be that they are hiding something in their car. Just look at the changes or signs of guilt.

Projectionism is a major weakness of the co narc. Because they cannot self-reflect since they cannot take blame, this is the only way they can really deal with the guilt. The guilt they have would injure their own ego if the victim committed those same crimes against the co narc. So look carefully. It is a gift for the victim, so don't overlook it and use it as a weapon.

Eventually, the co narc will become sloppy or slip up. They will do something that simply is out of bounds, and the victim will either stumble across the crime or someone else will point it out to them. This could be anything that the co narc and the victim both know is against their relationship rules. It could be a simple thing like raising the thermostat a couple of degrees to having an all-out affair. The victim will now confront the co narc, and this will cause major narcissistic injury.

Remember, the co narc cannot be wrong, nor can they never be seen as doing wrong. The co narc will almost, after denying, always get defensive and sometimes act out with narcissistic rage, something that is not pretty. One must realize what had just occurred.

The victim not only entered the *do-not-enter space* of the fragile house of cards but probably caused some damage to it. The co narc will now not know how to touch into their emotions or even try to self-reflect. The victim just put the co narc in a position that they just do not want to be. But they do not know how to process this information. Just like a cornered wounded animal, nobody knows exactly how they will react.

In a panic, the co narc will often lash out with rage. Physical violence, as ugly as it is, is often possible. Another possibility is the co narc will go on the offensive and often try to turn the tables on the victim. They may point out times in which the victim may have stepped out of line, like if the co narc spent a bit too much money or if they purchase something that they should not have. They may even point at the victim and blame them for their misdoings. It will be your fault that the co narc stepped out of line. You did not pay enough attention to the co narc, or you caused them to speed through the speed trap. It will and always will be a one-way relationship.

The co narc will not even acknowledge the trouble they may have caused. Remember, they simply cannot be wrong. The victim is wrong, and it does not matter whether the victim's feelings are hurt or destroyed. It is all about the feelings of the co narc.

Life after the Co Narc

Okay, the co narc is gone. The co narc discarded you, and now you face the world alone. If you were in the relationship for a good deal of time, you may find this time very strange and troubling because you simply are not used to it. At this point, you will be reaching out to family and friends for an ear to listen and for someone just to be there to give you comfort.

It will come to this point that you will now find out exactly who your true friends are. These are the ones that are there when you need them, the ones who will keep you going. The friends that come forward and are there for you are your true friends. They will want to be there for you. You will not need to ask for help.

You do not realize it, but you are now better off. But you do not know it because you do not know who you are and, more importantly, where your new boundaries are. No more walking through minefields, or always feeling afraid to take that next step. Now you have the ability to say anything you want without backlash and do things without penalties.

What does it mean to find out who you are? It sounds so simple and so basic; and some may, right after a discard, believe they know who they are but really do not. Just like that dog that lost one link of his chain each day while he was under the watch of the co narc. Now, its head is up against the doghouse. The dog will now gain one link each day.

Some may gain two or three links a day, and some may only get one link every two days. But the point here is the dog's boundaries will get greater. Soon, the dog will be able to reach the water bowl without choking themselves on the chain and drink whenever it wants, then it will be able to reach the grass where it could lay on comfortably instead of having to sit on the hard concrete and finally be able to reach its ball and play with it all it wants. Basically, a normal life.

Unfortunately, moving on will not be without some pain. If marriage is involved, the execution of divorce and splitting up all the assets are never fun. And if children are involved in the equation, it is very uncomfortable and must be handled with extreme care, not just in the immediate moment but also for some time.

If marriage is not the situation, I will not say the breakup will be any easier, but not dealing with lawyers and legal paper is a plus. You will remember the good times with the co narc, and in a strange way, you will miss them. Heck, you loved them. There was something you desired about them that attracted them to you. You will miss those good times.

The people around you will say, "Just forget them." But the problem is you will not only break the connection with them but you also had relationships with members of their community. Their family and friends were part of your life. You will miss spending New Year's Eve at their brother and wife's house. You will miss nieces and nephews who are innocent bystanders and whom you got so close to, but now, all those relationships are over.

Also, all your mutual friends unfortunately will be dragged into the fray. They will have to take sides and choose you or the co narc at times. They do not want to, but they have no choice. You will miss going out to see music in the park with your friends Glenn and Karen, and only because one of them is closer to your co narc, you will lose them as friends. In a strange way, some of your mutual friends will want no part of the split up and choose not to side with either one of you. They will become very uncomfortable with the situation and not reach out to either one of you, so they will disappear. Trust me, it hurts.

So suddenly, happening just overnight, your whole life is turned upside down and the world of mystery emerges. People do not enjoy the unknown; they do not feel comfortable when things are not predictable. People desire being in a realm that they are familiar with where life is predictable. And I believe this is where they really wish to return to. I believe they may miss the co narc on a certain level; but they miss the stability of the whole old life much more, not the unknown, which is what they are now facing, which they were forced into.

So now is time to heal. The breakup is fresh, and you are sorting things out. One thing I have learned by reading other survivors' stories online and in support groups is what happens when the co narc either comes back or wants to come back. And here is the kicker—they almost always try to. When the co narc calls or texts or shows up at the empath's doorstep, what do they do now? Or the co narc will at least try to test the water to see what their chances are and where they stand. They will hoover and set out feelers. Why? Why do they suddenly want to come back to a place that they found unacceptable before? You were the most undesirable person in the world. But now they want more; it does not make sense.

Why would they—after all the hell that they put you through, all the devaluing they did, the vicious discard, the lies—want to come back? They blamed you for everything. You were such a horrible person with all your faults. You could not screw in a light bulb correctly nor buy a decent Christmas gift. They were so unhappy.

The answer is simple. You are better than what they have now. Let us make that clear. They are tired of what they have now. The new supply is now the cowboy in black. You were a better car than the car they have now. You need a new wheel alignment, but the car they have now needs a new transmission. They are not finding the fill they need where they are now, or at least you were better. Also, if the relationship was for a good deal of time, the co narc will look for a person with the same qualities that you had.

They will hold you as the standard. And with all that you put up with, the bar is set high, higher than most new supplies are willing to put up with. They will expect the same or better treatment with the new supply but will have lower patience in getting it. And most people are not going to deal with this.

And remember, the co narc hates to be alone. Firstly, they hate themselves. So they do not like being alone with themselves. They gain no satisfaction when nobody is around feeding them. So they always want someone around. Do not let it be you. Give this problem to some other poor unsuspecting slob.

They will promise they will change, and they will admit they know they were difficult to live with and promise things will be different. But take this to the bank, cash the check, and spend the money—they will not; nothing will change. They may be on their best behavior for a short while, and they will start the love bombing again. The chemicals in your brain will be in abundance. But the sleeping ogre will show its ugly face again before the victim knows it.

Now, should the co narc be taken back? Of all the dozens of stories I have read and all the poor souls who try and try again and take them back, guess what, it never ends well. There is a zero chance of them changing and a zero chance the empath will be happy. Remember, there is no cure for narcissism. They entered the manipulation realm again, and remember, they are good at it. They know how to pull the sympathy strings. And they will love bomb you until they find a new fill.

Then the cycle starts all over again. And you will be hurt to a greater degree. Not only will you get hurt again, but you are wasting your time instead of moving on. And part of the reason for them to come back is not so you can feed them, but they do not want you to move on. They do not want to give a chance that you will find someone else and become happy. You must be miserable like them. Remember, you can become happy; they cannot. You love yourself; they do not. There is a load of good people out there, people who will make you very happy. So go out there and get one.

The research I have read suggested the best way to move on from the co narc is to go what is called no contact. It is exactly what the name implies. Do not communicate with them, do not answer their text messages, do not answer their phone call, and do not meet up with them. They do not deserve any of your attention. They do not have feelings for you, and as soon as you figure that out, it will be easy.

You will feel good when they contact you, and you do even feel bad not answering them. Knowing that you are causing discomfort to them, it is satisfying. Does it affect them? Yes, because now, something that was a sure thing is no longer there. They now feel a bit more isolated. A narcissist hates being rejected. Remember, zero contact.

I realize sometimes that communication with them in unavoidable due to children, work, or other scenarios. This will be less effective for no contact, but you should now resort to something called gray rock. No, it is not finding the biggest gray rock and throwing it at them. As much as you may want to do, I do not suggest this. What gray rocking is, is communicating with them only what is necessary. Keep it to that subject alone.

Do not answer questions like "How are you doing?" or "Remember when we went to the beach?" They dumped you. Say goodbye.

Good Luck

I certainly hope this book has helped you understand or at least will set you in the right direction to a path of sanity. Once you are over the shock of the discard, you will start to reflect. You will start to understand why things happened and wonder why you were so blind. You will beat yourself up for the times when you believed. You may have overreacted or have not handled situations correctly and got angry when you felt you were taken advantage of or did not react enough. Understanding what and why this happened to you will make things easier to digest.

Unfortunately, as I have learned after speaking to other narcissist survivors, reading and researching this disorder—either watching YouTube videos or reading this book—will call to mind uncomfortable and unwanted memories.

Remember, you do not have to walk this road alone, and most importantly, you should not be embarrassed or believe you are in a unique or unheard-of situation. I simply cannot overstress the importance of finding help. Lean on family members and friends when you are down and take advantage when you are feeling good. Those close to you probably saw the abuse or at least witnessed something unusual.

The amount of information on the internet is infinite. Each situation is different. We all have different personalities, upbringing, religious beliefs, and temperament; so healing will be different to all.

Professional help is a strong recommendation. The understanding of the disorder of narcissism is expanding. Very effective techniques to recover are being discovered constantly, so take advantage of them.

After all the insanity, it will take time to realize you are in a better place, so take it slow.

Ozzy Osbourne said, "And the weather is looking fine, and I think the sun will shine again." Trust me, it will.

About the Author

Mike was born in Brooklyn and was raised on Long Island. He launched his flying career in 1989 as a flight engineer for TWA. For the last nineteen years, he has successfully flown for American Airlines and was promoted to captain in 2019. In his spare time, Mike loves to carve pieces of wood, transforming them into beautiful household objects.

He is fascinated by the Civil War and airplane engines and is able to fix most anything he lays his hands on. Mike was married for thirty years. He is now divorced and in a loving and healthy relationship. He raised two wonderful sons, Michael and Andrew.

9 798888 763222 3